MADE
FOR
LIVING

MADE
FOR
LIVING

COLLECTED INTERIORS FOR
ALL SORTS OF STYLES

AMBER LEWIS
with
CAT CHEN

PHOTOGRAPHS BY
TESSA NEUSTADT

CLARKSON POTTER/PUBLISHERS
NEW YORK

Copyright © 2020 by AMBER LEWIS
Photographs © 2020 by TESSA NEUSTADT

Published in the United States by Clarkson Potter/Publishers, an imprint
of Random House, a division of Penguin Random House LLC, New York.
clarksonpotter.com

CLARKSON POTTER is a trademark and POTTER with colophon is a registered trademark of
Penguin Random House LLC.

Library of Congress Cataloging-in-Publication Data
Names: Lewis, Amber, author. | Neustadt, Tessa, photographer (expression)
Title: Made for living : collected interiors for all sorts of styles / Amber Lewis ; photographs
    by Tessa Neustadt.
Description: First edition. | New York : Clarkson Potter/Publishers, 2020.
Identifiers: LCCN 2019053004 (print) | LCCN 2019053005 (ebook) |
    ISBN 9781984823915 | ISBN 9781984823922 (ebook)
Subjects: LCSH: Interior decoration.
Classification: LCC NK2115 .L44 2020 (print) | LCC NK2115 (ebook) |
    DDC 747—dc23
LC record available at https://lccn.loc.gov/2019053004
LC ebook record available at https://lccn.loc.gov/2019053005

ISBN 978-1-9848-2391-5
Ebook ISBN 978-1-9848-2392-2

Printed in China

Book and cover design by SONIA PERSAD
Photography by TESSA NEUSTADT
Photography on pages 70, 71, 102, 103, and 216 (bottom left) by JESS ISAAC.

20 19 18 17 16

First Edition

CONTENTS

INTRODUCTION

How do I get your look?

As an interior designer and a lifestyle blogger, I'm asked a lot of questions, and how to translate my style is the one I get asked most. By now, "my look" has become distinct enough that I like to think if you viewed a police lineup of five different homes you'd instantly identify the one I designed. That said, you might not be able to easily sum it up in a few words. Even *I* struggle with that, because my look isn't about one thing or the other but rather it's a specific mix that I've spent years developing.

I don't believe in being monogamous to one design vibe. If you're looking for a rule book and guide to the "right" way to design a home, *Made for Living* isn't it. But if you want to develop a personal approach to interior style that feels as if it grew up out of the ground, rather than bought or prescribed—well, then, you've come to the right place. Get ready for spaces that feel both fresh and current but also layered and approachable, homes with finishes that are tactile and rooted in nature, and furniture that effortlessly mixes flea market finds and sleeker shapes in a blend that feels like it will last forever. My kind of elusive, laid-back California cool can be had anywhere—whether you live in a Manhattan apartment or in the middle of suburbia.

You can take the title of this book literally: Everything in these pages is really made for *living*. In the rooms I design, the sofas are matched with beautiful ottomans upholstered in tactile fabrics that, yes, you can actually put your feet up on (or, in my case, Converse). In my own kitchen, I used one of my favorite materials:

beautiful, variegated Moroccan glazed terra-cotta tiles. They're full of nicks and dings; no two pieces are alike. And that's why I love them. "Perfect" is not my goal.

Livability is my true north. I don't want you to worry about constantly fluffing your pillows. I gravitate toward things that look better with time, pieces that feel like they have stories of their own. I hoard vintage finds because I love a true patina that can't be re-created in a factory. And the materials I use time and again—linens and leathers, brass fixtures, honed marble, white oak flooring—they all change over time. The way your sofa looks on the day it gets delivered is not the way it will look in a few years. Not only is that okay, that's a good thing. That's how you achieve more than a re-creation of what you've already seen, or what somebody else has. You can do this, too—I promise.

To those who ask me *how* to get my look, *Made for Living* is for you. Full of tips and tricks and know-how, the book breaks down the building blocks of my signature style and delves into my design thought process and the "rules" I've developed along the way (which is often by breaking tired, old-school conventions).

More important, my goal is to inspire you to use my favorite elements to create a look that feels distinctly yours—and to show you how to apply them in your space, making it feel unique to you.

In every interior I design, I see different aspects of my own life coming together to form an aesthetic. This began when I was ten years old, the age when a person begins to become aware of their "happy place" in the world. I found mine when my family moved to Malibu, California. Now, I was no spoiled rich kid. Ours was not the stereotypical Malibu of cheesy TV shows. We didn't drive fancy cars or live in a crazy mansion. On the contrary, my parents were California hippies before that was anointed "California chic," and our version of Malibu was a wonderfully intimate, low-key seaside community—one you rarely hear about these days.

My mother was a stay-at-home mom, always cooking or crafting, organizing our schedules, and keeping us busy learning and creating, pushing us to draw or play outside instead of plopping us in front of screens. My dad is a contractor who prides himself on "putting on his bags" and getting to work—his "bags" being the battered leather tool belt he wore with trashed skate shoes and shorts, no matter the weather. Even though he owns his business, he loves the feeling of tools in his hands, actually doing the work. Manual labor was never beneath him, and that tireless work ethic—and respect for the integrity of craftsmanship—has been ingrained in me.

My brother, sister, and I grew up walking on the beach collecting shells and white, heart-shaped rocks while our dad surfed the waves. But for me, the beach was less about the sand and the shells than it was about the view—I needed an open end. Our house had unobstructed views of the Pacific; from the balcony, you could see the whole coast, from sand to horizon, and the occasional whale surfacing in the distance. Growing up surrounded by the colors and textures of nature, noticing the way the light danced on the water and changed with the seasons, and how this affected my mood—all of this played a huge role in who I am as a person. I felt happiest when I had horizons, a never-ending blue abyss in front of me. I got attached to nature from that perspective. Today, that sense of unobstructed light and air is my foundation.

THE BOOK BREAKS DOWN THE BUILDING BLOCKS OF MY SIGNATURE STYLE AND DELVES INTO MY DESIGN THOUGHT PROCESS.

In the earthy rugs and textiles I source for every project, I see myself in my teens and twenties, beginning to explore the world. Truth: I hated school. I started working at fifteen, and though I stayed in high school till I graduated at seventeen, I had an itch to see more. So the moment I got my driver's license, at age sixteen, I did what you do when you grow up in LA: I hit the Pacific Coast Highway (a.k.a. the PCH). In California, I've always been transfixed by how you can fly an hour in one direction, or drive five hours in another, and find yourself in completely different worlds. I love that I can jump from snowy mountains to forested lakes and rivers to some of the most beautiful beaches on Earth, yet somehow I always know I'm in California. This notion—consistency without uniformity—is the cornerstone of how I approach putting rooms together.

At seventeen, I lit out, traveling all over Europe, desperate to see what lay outside my small, beloved Malibu bubble. At twenty-two, I met my husband, a musician, and with him I toured the world, hitting almost every country in Europe, as well as Japan, and beyond. Everywhere we went, I was collecting mental images. I was fascinated by the local design—whether it was the ancient materials and craftsmanship in a French antiques market or the minimal, streamlined timelessness of Scandinavian design. It all stuck with me.

As you might be gathering by now, design is not something I was taught or learned in school. I am a grade-A dropout, friends. When I was twenty-three and about a year into a well-known interior design program, the universe offered up a mini miracle: a job as a design assistant at a small firm. I'm rarely one to take the sensible, linear path. By the time this opportunity came knocking, I'd already been on a somewhat bumpy and randomly plotted trajectory, working as a personal assistant, a salesperson, a window-display designer, an event planner, a florist. Hell, I've even dabbled in creating murals and painted a few houses.

THE PROCESS OF DESIGNING A HOME CAN BE INTENSE, BUT I'M HERE TO HELP MAKE SENSE OF IT FOR YOU.

At the time, my design training had just begun in earnest. Leaving school was risky. But I believed that I had a real eye. And the job seemed like a fast track to actually doing the work I loved. So I decided to wing it. Working in interior design without formal training isn't easy—in fact, it's something I rarely recommend to up-and-comers. I had to work extra hard, learning on my feet to make up for the formal skills I lacked. But as an interior design assistant, I was a sponge, devouring design magazines and books and studying fabric samples. Even as I sourced items that aligned with my boss's aesthetic, I was beginning to curate my own, daydreaming about how I'd have designed each house myself.

It was not exactly smooth sailing to get to where I am now. The seed for what is now Amber Interiors was planted the day I got fired from that assistant job. Around the same time, my daughter, Gwyneth, was born, and my husband's career as a touring musician was coming to an end. We'd just bought our first house, in LA, and I decided to start a blog documenting our home renovation and DIY projects. Soon I had plunged full steam ahead into my own interior design business.

Starting a business is hard. Starting a business when you are also caring for an eighteen-month-old is *really* hard. Starting a business when you are caring for an eighteen-month-old, experiencing postpartum depression, and have a husband who is transitioning out of the job that provides your family's monthly income feels *so hard* you are convinced you will die of stress-induced injuries.

To say that things were crazy? That would be an understatement.

Only now can I see the luck in this series of events. Hardship fueled my fire. It's what triggered the course of my life, the kick in the pants I needed to turn what could have been a sob story into a life I'm proud of and feel compelled to share with others daily. If you'd told me ten years ago that what started as a modest blog would mushroom into a multifaceted business that now includes a thriving design firm and retail stores, I'd never have believed you. And if you'd told me that by 2020, I'd be publishing a book about my "signature style," I would literally have laughed out loud. But I couldn't be more thrilled to share what I've learned with you in these pages.

It's taken me years to identify who I am as a designer and define what makes my style, *my style*. My hope for you, reader, is that you will not only absorb my tricks of the trade but also hear and internalize the stories behind the spaces I've designed—the spirit of the thing—and then filter the advice and the stories through your own lived experience, your taste, your vision. The process of designing a home can be intense, but I'm here to help make sense of it for you. Ready to get started?

THE
POWER
OF
COLOR

I WAS SIX YEARS OLD WHEN I TACKLED MY FIRST BIG
DECORATING PROJECT WITH A CAPITAL *P*. WE HAD MOVED
INTO A NEW HOUSE—A FIXER-UPPER—AND, AS PART OF THE
REMODEL, MY DAD WAS ADDING A SECOND STORY FOR ALL OF
OUR BEDROOMS. MY MOM HAD GIVEN ME THE OPPORTUNITY
TO PICK THE DÉCOR SCHEME FOR MY NEW BEDROOM.

I specifically remember being ecstatic about choosing the paint color for my walls
and I was hell-bent on having a pink room. For me, it was less about surrounding
myself with the stereotypical girly colors and more about establishing the right vibe
for my room. I remember feeling so certain of not only how I wanted my room
to *look*, but also how I wanted it to make me and others *feel*. I just knew the color
pink would genuinely make me feel happier, and I felt confident my friends would
agree. I don't really know how or why at the ripe old age of six I was so certain of my
personal color theory, or why I *knew* so distinctly how pink would affect my general
well-being, but I did. I was all about how a space, or a color, or a vibe made me feel
and, to this day, choosing colors based on an overall vibe and feeling is still a huge
factor in my design process.

While these days pink speaks to me a lot less than a beautiful neutral does, my
philosophy that color should make you *feel* something still rings true to my core.
Color is powerful in this way. The next time you decide to paint or repaint your walls,
try tuning into your younger self and asking what he or she might do. If you take any
lesson from this chapter, it's that picking a paint color should be fun—and I mean
really fun. Now, after several years of trial and error, I have a time-tested formula for
selecting paint. Read on to take in lessons I have learned … from age six 'til now!

We wanted to go all out with a girly-girl vibe in this little girl's room, so I chose a blush colorway in the shibori-style wallpaper I designed.

PAINT

Since starting my design firm and writing my blog, I have been getting a lot of questions, like "What colors belong in the same palette?" or "How can you mix different hues of one color in a room?" or "Does picking the right white paint actually matter?" All valid questions that, after royally flubbing up a few times, I almost feel qualified to answer. The truth is, I may have changed my mind about a color or two, once or twice, after picking a color palette. Guess what? That is totally okay. Part of designing is about experimenting with colors. It's about trial and error. I don't advise painting the entire exterior of your home a color that you might not be sure about, but on a much smaller scale, it's smart to play with a few options before you go all in on one shade.

When I start the decorating portion of a project, picking a color palette is one of the first things I do to get the party started. This is quite possibly one of the most challenging parts of the process because color in general—and paint specifically—greatly affects the way a person experiences a space. If you screw up the paint, you might screw up the whole room! I am not gonna sugarcoat it folks, 'cause the pressure is real. Of course, I don't mean to scare you, but this decision makes me feel the most vulnerable. It's usually one of the first things contractors need to know before they begin, because if you are painting the trim or ceilings, or adding wallpaper, they need to factor that into their budget and scope of work.

When working with an open layout, try using multiple paint colors in complementary tones for your trim, walls, and cabinetry so everything connects.

RIGHT   A fresh coat of Simply
White by Benjamin Moore helped
brighten up the reclaimed brick
flooring in this space.

OPPOSITE   This room features
all Dunn-Edwards paint: White
Heat covers the walls and ceilings,
and Midnight Spruce makes a
statement on the kitchen cabinets.

You may be thinking, "Praise you, designer lady, for helping me survive this décor decision hell." Or you might be scratching your head wondering, "Girl, who even cares?" Well I do, because picking the right paint matters one hundred percent. It's the base layer and backdrop for the whole shebang. Every single design and décor decision will need to complement the color on the walls. Trust me when I say I have had to repaint a few walls in my lifetime because they didn't quite turn out the way I wanted them to, or the color just didn't feel right. Lucky for you, I've already made the mistakes, so I hope to save you a step or two in this chapter. Okay, great, now let's make sure we get the right color on your walls. Sound good?

Benjamin Moore's White Dove contrasts nicely with the stained wood exterior.
Petit Granit limestone countertops and black pendants help tie it all together.

HOW TO NAIL PAINT EVERY TIME

THE KEY IS PATIENCE. THIS PART OF THE PROCESS TAKES TIME. IT'S WORTH EVERY PAINSTAKING SECOND TO GET THIS RIGHT, SO BEAR WITH ME AND DON'T SAY I DIDN'T WARN YOU.

- Take a full assessment of the room and determine how much the light affects the space throughout the day. The questions you should be asking yourself are: Do you live in a more cave-like home or do you reside in a big glass box? Simply put, how much light does your space get? Where does the sun rise and set? What is the quality of light? For example, do you get heavy morning sun, but no sun by midday? Or are you flooded with natural light all day and need to tone it down a bit?

- Consider your surroundings, both inside and out. Take note of the floors, countertops, and built-in fixtures inside the space. When you look outside, what do you see? Are you surrounded by greenery or a cityscape? These existing elements will reflect their color against your paint selections–especially white paint--and can affect the shade drastically.

- Play with sheens. Fact 1: The more luster a paint has, the lighter it will look and the more wall blemishes and defects the paint will reflect. If shiny is your vibe, then you have to get your surface smooth and clear. This is a laborious process: you should be sure every inch of whatever you are painting—be it walls, trim, ceilings, or furniture—is thoroughly prepped and ready for shine.

- Once you narrow your selection, paint large samples (at least 24 x 24 inches) on the walls you want to cover. Alternatively, use my method: Paint a few sample boards in different colors and scatter them around a room.

- Live with those samples for a couple of days and watch how they change throughout the day and into the night. If you've painted sample boards, you can continuously move them around. Until you pay attention, you may not realize just how the light will change in your home. You want to eliminate the possibility of choosing a color that you love in the morning but end up hating in the evening.

- This goes without saying, but don't forget to consider the tones of the room's furniture and décor. Choose a paint that complements your color palette. Pull out fabric swatches and compare them to the paint in the room to see if all the tones work together.

Not too cold and not too yellow: it was a no-brainer to use my ultimate Goldilocks neutral, Simply White by Benjamin Moore, to add warmth and make the space feel more inviting.

This room from the house I call Bu Round Two features
Directors Cut by Portola Paints in a plaster finish called
Roman Clay. The delicate texture and depth of the plaster
made this extremely large entryway feel cozier.

THE DEAL WITH WHITE PAINT

Now let's focus our attention on white paint specifically. As a designer known for my frequent use of this particular hue in my projects, I know how a poorly chosen shade of white can throw off the entire feel of a space. And if you are thinking, "What's the big deal? White paint is white paint," then I am here to tell you otherwise. There's no such thing as "white paint." There are a million different whites, and no two are the same. Each brand has its own formula for creating paint, and each color has its own unique undertone. Lay out ten different swatches of white paint next to one another, and you'll see how drastically different they are. Understanding a few common terms we use in the industry to describe colors can be helpful:

- *Mass or overall tone.* This is the general color you see and identify immediately. For example, if you look at a green-painted wall, you would describe that mass tone as green.

- *Undertone.* This is the base tone of a color. You may hear designers say, "It's a very yellow white" or "That white reads blue." This means that the color has been mixed with tints to help develop a variation in the color itself.

- *Warm tones.* Pigments derived from warm color tones—red, orange, and yellow—are mixed with white to get warmer results. If a white is "warm" it can often be described as "creamy."

- *Cool tones.* Cooler colors, like blue, green, and magenta, tint a color to produce a colder-feeling white.

LEFT AND CENTER   Both of these rooms from two different houses feature my go-to, Simply White by Benjamin Moore.

OPPOSITE   This bungalow features Milk Glass by Dunn-Edwards.

OVERLEAF   On the list of my favorite neutral whites is Milk Glass by Dunn-Edwards. We wanted a very bright white for this living room, but we shied away from using anything too blue or cold. In some lights, this color can lean green, so we followed one of my rules and took the outside into consideration; we chose the hue because it didn't seem to reflect any landscape green indoors.

So, is there a specific formula to keep from going too cold or too warm? Unfortunately, the answer is not black and white, and many factors determine my choices. There are a few general rules that do help me decide, though. For example, I'll probably start by considering the style and vibe I'm looking to achieve. If it's a Spanish-style home, I'll opt for something a bit on the warmer side because I know I'll be incorporating some darker, earthier pieces. If I'm going for midcentury, Scandinavian modern, I'll likely go for something on the cooler side, because I want the space to feel fresh and bright but certainly not too cold.

I'll also consider how much natural light fills the space. When sunlight streams through the windows, it reflects against floors, furniture, and rugs then bounces back onto the walls. For that reason, I tend to stick to warmer or more neutral tones when designing spaces flooded with natural light. By choosing a warmer neutral tone, the space will feel naturally brighter when the sun shines in.

FOR REALZ THE NICEST PEOPLE ON THE PLANET

Let me spin you a tale, my friends, of a time in which choosing a white paint for a project was quite tricky, and my team ultimately conquered by going warm. When working on one of my absolute favorite projects, which I call For Realz the Nicest People on the Planet, located in Lafayette, California, we ran into a few big challenges. Among architect Barbara Chambers, the homeowners, and me, we knew we wanted a bright, all-white space. The only issue was that meant that there would be *a lot* of white. My biggest challenge was landing on a color that complemented the light-filled space, but not one that would make the house feel sterile or unintentionally cold. Specifically, our goal was to find the perfect white that was warm enough to tone down all the natural light flooding in through the windows, make the space feel cozy despite the sixteen-foot cathedral ceilings, and not read too yellow with the bounce of tones coming from the natural oak floors. To add another challenge into the mix, we had to deal with a house full of glass and windows—not to mention fog and the seasons—which meant the light would change every minute of the day. We knew the sky would change and bring out a different hue in the house! With all these factors, we went down a paint wormhole.

I knew the only way to fix this was to get swatching, and swatch we did. If we were going to achieve the charming, effortless, modern farmhouse vibe I was going for, patience was key, and painting a ton of samples on the wall would be the critical step. As with all my projects, we started by painting numerous swatches on boards and moving them around the house. We tried different colors and sheens, focusing on hues that had tints of brown with a little bit of yellow to help warm up the home. The clients and I checked back on them throughout the day to see

Because of the abundance of natural light in every room,
White Dove by Benjamin Moore was the clear winner for
the majority of this house. This paint color can often read
a little yellow, but in this case it ended up balancing all the
sunlight to be the perfect neutral.

how they changed, and we asked the on-site project manager to take a couple of pictures during different times of day to capture the changing light. Most of the time, the white hues we chose all seemed to work great in the morning, but we pretty much despised them by the afternoon. As annoying as that was for everyone, I knew it was a worthwhile exercise. We had to eliminate the colors that didn't work and narrow down the winners. We persevered and it paid off.

I ended up choosing White Dove by Benjamin Moore throughout the majority of the house. For anyone familiar with this color, it can read *very* warm, maybe even yellow to some, but for this house and its natural lighting, White Dove was our ideal neutral. Something about this house picked up on the slight undertones of a warm gray and showed almost zero yellow or blue tones. Plus, the color stayed relatively consistent throughout the day. It ended up being a win-win-win for us. This color is now a go-to for me.

But as with most things in design, the stars don't always align, and we had a very stubborn room: the family room/TV den. This space is located just off the main great room but in an area of the house that did not receive as much direct natural light. All the same requirements I outlined above applied here when choosing the paint color. We still wanted the space to feel cozy, but we needed a white that was inherently livelier to help compensate for that lack of light without the color feeling like a departure from the rest of the house. In order to cheer up the space, I ended up choosing a brighter complementary shade, Simply White by Benjamin Moore. This particular shade still maintained a neutral undertone without making the room feel cold. By choosing something a couple of shades lighter than White Dove, we achieved that perfect, fresh white.

The TV den had less natural light, so we opted for Simply White by Benjamin Moore to give it the brightness it was lacking.

A bright-as-can-be family room was the perfect candidate to continue the White Dove paint scheme. Our neutral and tonal selection of furniture and vintage pieces grounded this room with just the right amount of warmth.

41

MY GO-TO WHITE PAINTS

TO SAVE YOU SOME DECISION MAKING, HERE ARE MY PREFERRED WHITE PAINTS AND WHEN TO USE EACH ONE.

THE ALL-AROUND WINNER

- *Wevet by Farrow & Ball*

  PROS: The prettiest, warmest white. I use this to bring warmth to any space.

  CONS: It can go a little beige and yellow if paired with a brighter white trim. Try painting the trim the same color as the walls for a tonal and serene look.

NICE NEUTRALS

- *Milk Glass by Dunn-Edwards*

  PROS: Like its name, this has a very milky and fresh feel to it. I painted all the walls in my last house this color!

  CONS: It can read green in certain lights. Avoid painting it in rooms where green grass or a blue pool could reflect inside.

- *Simply White by Benjamin Moore*

  PROS: This is a very versatile and true neutral white. It's ideal for most rooms, especially ones with less natural light. To be honest, I play favorites with this shade and have had few complaints about it.

  CONS: It can go a little warm if paired with a stark white trim. Avoid pairing anything with a cool undertone.

THE BEST WARM WHITES

- *White Dove by Benjamin Moore*

  PROS: This is a warm white with a beige undertone. It looks great in a room with larger windows and a steady stream of light throughout the day.

Simpy White by Benjamin Moore is as true a neutral white as it gets. This entryway had less natural light than the rest of the house, and this white helped revitalize the space.

CONS: Be mindful of using this color for cabinets. The same is true if you have a gray-toned marble or quartz countertop, because it can end up reading dull or dirty next to anything with a cool tone.

- *Wimborne White by Farrow & Ball*
PROS: This is a moody white, if you will. It's great in a Spanish-style home or if you want a space to feel like it has some history, but it's definitely not my pick for a contemporary or modern home.

CONS: This can read very yellow and may not be a bright enough white if there is not enough natural light. Don't use it in a room without windows, like a powder room.

- *White Heat by Dunn-Edwards*
PROS: This paint is warm, warm, warm! I'll put it this way: If beige, vanilla cream, and sunshine had a perfectly neutral paint baby, it would be this color.

CONS: Similar to Wimborne White, this shade can go yellow if there is not enough natural light or if the space is surrounded by red-toned floors.

- *Whisper by Dunn-Edwards*
PROS: This is light and warm and looks great with dark or light floors.

CONS: As with a lot of my warmer paint choices, it can have some unflattering yellow undertones, so be wary of using it next to white drapery.

A warm, warm white that works just right, White Heat by Dunn-Edwards features throughout the entire home of What's the Story, Spanish Glory?

When you're working with tonal and earthy colors in the rest of the décor, try a neutral white to balance all of the warmth. Here's another example of Milk Glass by Dunn-Edwards.

PERFECT COOL WHITES

- *Cool December by Dunn-Edwards*
  PROS: A very fresh and clean shade of white with undertones of blue and cool gray. If you want some stark white walls, this is your color.

  CONS: Make sure you check how this color looks on a foggy day or early morning when the light is dim. This shade can feel sterile if not paired with a warmer floor color or neutral palette.

- *Chantilly Lace by Benjamin Moore*
  PROS: This is a cool-toned and crisp white. Its hints of green and gray will easily brighten a dark space.

  CONS: Avoid painting this in a bathroom. The green and blue tones are not great in rooms with mirrors!

- *Snow White by Benjamin Moore*
  PROS: With its undertones of gray, green, and a bit of blue, I like this paint for a more modern-style home.

  CONS: This shade has the tendency to read sterile, so make sure to choose a décor and color palette that can balance it.

Here's Cool December by Dunn-Edwards in a room where a fresh white with cool undertones was the name of the game.

The color White by Dunn-Edwards is a perfect clean and bright white, ideal for midcentury-style homes like this one. To no surprise, we used this paint throughout the entire home.

WHITE TRIM

- *White by Dunn-Edwards*
  The perfect clean and bright trim. Enough
  said. I like to use this in a velvet or satin
  sheen because it has a slight luster to it
  without it feeling too shiny.

- *Decorator's White by Benjamin Moore*
  For decorators, this is a cult classic. It's a
  stereotypical bright white, a great backdrop
  for many things. I like this on cabinets, trim,
  millwork, and ceilings.

- *Foggy Day by Dunn-Edwards*
  If you're looking to flip the switch a bit and
  paint the trim a slightly darker, contrasting
  color, this is one of my go-to grays. It stands
  out ever so slightly against white walls.

RIGHT   Decorator's White by Benjamin Moore is
cheery and versatile; we used it for every part of this
home, including the walls, ceilings, and trim.

OVERLEAF   We chose Milk Glass by Dunn-Edwards
for this Malibu bungalow.

THE POWER OF
DARK PAINT

As much as I love working with an all-white room, I am equally drawn to a dark and saturated backdrop. Whether it's the color of the wall, dark-painted cabinetry, or a piece of furniture, when done right, a dark paint color will stop you in your tracks. From black and deep blues to wine and olive green, these dramatic hues can set a tone that is moody, unexpected, and powerful while layering on depth, contrast, and character.

I want to set the record straight about painting walls dark. I love a good fable more than anyone, but I must debunk the myth that if you paint your walls with anything darker than white or light gray, your room will look cramped. It's simply not true. I apologize for whoever started that nasty rumor, because lo and behold, some of my much-loved rooms to date are dark and moody and still feel spacious. I have tried this in small powder rooms, master bedrooms, dining rooms, studies, mudrooms, kitchens—you name it—and it's worked like a charm every time!

Maison by Portola Paints in Roman Clay plaster finish amps up the drama in this small powder room. The stone-like gray mixed with the reclaimed limestone sink creates a texture combo made in heaven.

Amherst Gray by Benjamin Moore
stops you in your tracks when used
as boldly as we applied it in this
house I call Canyon Cool.

ABOVE   We carried on with dark paint in the powder room at Canyon Cool. Here you see Anchor Gray by Benjamin Moore, offset by a marble floating sink with steel-gray veining.

OPPOSITE   Over in the study room at Canyon Cool, we opted for Black Pool by Dunn-Edwards, a daringly deep black with a hint of dark green. To offset the moodiness, we added a rich, faded rug and a stone-gray sofa.

THE COMBO OF DARK
PIECES IN A LIGHT-FILLED
ROOM INSTANTLY CREATES
A FOCAL POINT.

ABOVE   This room floods with natural light,
and it was begging for some drama. Stained
pine custom cabinetry against the white wall
and a striking piece of art gave this room the
extra ambiance it needed.

OPPOSITE   The kitchen and staircase in
Black Houses Are the Best Houses.

Not convinced? There are ways to add mood without feeling all the saturation scaries. Adding dark colors to a bright white room doesn't always feel intuitive; you might think it's too much of a contrast, but trust me on this one: The combo of dark pieces in a light-filled room instantly creates a focal point, even if it's just a statement piece like a dining table or cabinetry. Take, for example, my design for Black Houses Are the Best Houses, a Scandinavian-inspired house in Venice, California. Since the exterior of the house was predominantly stained black, I carried elements of the hue throughout the interior as well in the form of built-in metal kitchen cabinetry and structural beams.

We chose Black Lead by Dunn-Edwards for all the kitchen and pantry cabinets in this home, adding an elegant vibe to a naturally bright room.

Featuring the paint color Jet from Dunn-Edwards, this island helps
visually section off the kitchen in an open-concept space.

DARK PAINTS I DEPEND ON

- *Green Black by Sherwin-Williams*
  An almost-black with a green undertone that looks amazing on a front door or kitchen cabinets.

- *Nitty Gritty by Portola Paints*
  If you want to add some interesting texture to your space, start small and go for a powder room or your child's bedroom with this amazing blue-green plaster clay specialty paint.

- *Black Pool by Dunn-Edwards*
  Is it black or is it dark navy? Actually, it's both! This color is first on our list for painting millwork in a library and can be a perfect accent color on a bathroom vanity.

- *Down Pipe by Farrow & Ball*
  This color is the perfect combo of a blue-black and gray master mix on anything from cabinetry to an exterior. This one is hard to get wrong, so paint it on everything and never look back.

- *Maison by Portola Paints*
  Another texture-friendly option, a deep gray with subtle hints of blue mix that's perfectly dramatic.

The cabinetry in this kitchen features Down Pipe by Farrow & Ball.

Thanks to Green Black by Sherwin-Williams,
this kitchen ended up edgy and elevated yet
traditional and laid-back.

THE EVERYTHING-
IN-BETWEEN COLORS

It's true: I love white, black, and all the neutral and earthy tones I can get my hands on. That said, it is just as important for any room to have a pop of color here and there. Color speaks to people and deeply affects the way we feel. While I'm not personally drawn to highlighter bright colors, I will never tire of a light pink room or a classic pop of red. When it comes to the colors in between black and white, I will always love my greens and blues, with rusts and bits of saffron mixed in.

Kitchen cabinetry has always been one of my go-to ways to add a unique or unexpected color. If I don't choose a lighter tone for cabinetry, then I almost always gravitate toward a deep saturated hue. I absolutely love the way darker-painted cabinets give such a visual contrast to whatever space you are trying to highlight. If you can be so bold and get down with the moody vibes of a darker paint, it can really take a space to the next level. A great example of where I chose to bring in a unique color to set the tone of the house and make the kitchen feel super special was in the kitchen of Oh Hi Ojai.

We set out to bring earthy Ojai colors into this home, which made Midnight Spruce by Dunn-Edwards—a dark forest green with hints of olive—the choice for this cabinetry.

Another view of the kitchen from the home Oh Hi Ojai, where we brought many colors and elements from outdoors inside.

RIGHT   For the bathroom, we
went with Black Pool by Dunn-
Edwards.

OPPOSITE   The solid oak
shelving and oak floors pull in
other elements from the outside,
like trees and good ol' dirt.

OVERLEAF   For this family
kitchen, we went with Benjamin
Moore paint: Revere Pewter for
the cabinetry and Wrought Iron
for the kitchen island.

In my humble opinion, Ojai is one of the most magical places in California. It embodies all the wonderful things nature has to offer and holds a very special place in my heart. It's a serene and sweet town in a valley surrounded by beautiful mountains with sunsets to die for. Nature is everywhere, and the oak trees and rolling roads are stunning.

My client's home sat in an orchard, and the leaves on the fruit trees influenced a lot of the creativity behind the décor selection. When choosing the color Midnight Spruce for the cabinets, I wanted all those incredible natural colors and earthy elements found in the immediate environment to be reflected on the inside of the home. The homeowners wanted the space to feel special and put together, but also inviting and down to earth. They got precisely that.

TOP IN-BETWEEN PAINTS

WHEN I'M FEELING LIKE A ROOM NEEDS A LITTLE EXTRA SOMETHING, I START WITH THESE STATEMENT PAINT COLORS.

- *Midnight Spruce by Dunn-Edwards*
  As used in Oh Hi Ojai's kitchen cabinetry, this is a dark forest green with a hint of olive that makes this color a classic for painting cabinetry or furniture pieces.
- *Manor House Gray by Farrow & Ball*
  A dramatic, true gray. No matter the lighting in your space, this gray will hold its hue.
- *Purbeck Stone by Farrow & Ball*
  A calming gray that gives me serious British design vibes.
- *Revere by Portola Paints*
  A gorgeous gray with hints of blue and green and all the texture you'd ever need.
- *Hague Blue by Farrow & Ball*
  A statement-making deep blue that I find to be timeless and a little moody.

The built-ins in this playroom feature Manor House Gray by Farrow & Ball.

Shady by Dunn-Edwards is a nice feathery gray for this kitchen cabinetry: it's modern and traditional and adds to that California cool you know I love so much.

WHEN TO GO WITH WALLPAPER

There are times when a simple ol' painted wall won't quite do the trick. Sometimes, you need more color, more texture, and more pattern, and I think one of the easiest ways to achieve that is by adding wallpaper. It instantly adds personality to a room.

I have used wallpaper on numerous occasions, both subtly and not so subtly. One example of my restrained applications of wallpaper was in the living room of West Coast Is the Best Coast (overleaf). As you already know, I love white rooms, but, even for me, this room was a bit too pale, and I needed a solution to warm up the very large space. Because the floor in this room was a darker wood and the ceiling was painted white, I needed something to break up the stark difference between the two. I decided on a beautiful, creamy but beigy, gray-toned wallpaper to sit above the chair rail to do exactly that. Although the wallpaper was technically pretty "neutral," the textured material added a layer of warmth and coziness that was really necessary.

OPPOSITE   Here is a more traditional use of wallpaper, where pattern adds movement throughout the room.

OVERLEAF   Wallpaper isn't always about pattern. It can add texture in the most subtle yet powerful ways. Here, white painted walls felt too stark, so we opted for a textured, creamy beige wallpaper to warm up the living room at West Coast Is the Best Coast.

IT'S ALL

IN THE

DETAILS

ONCE YOU'VE DECIDED ON YOUR COLOR PALETTE, THE NEXT STEP BEFORE YOU EVEN START CHOOSING FURNITURE OR FABRICS IS TO THINK ABOUT THE BONES OF THE ROOM. THIS MEANS THE HARDWARE FINISHES, MATERIALS, TILES, AND ALL THE SMALL THINGS IN BETWEEN.

Now's the time to consider each and every detail to make sure everything works. I have meetings with my clients just to go over material options, and sometimes those meetings can last for days. There is a lot of ground to cover when it comes to the little things, and if they get overlooked, it's a major bummer once the whole room comes together.

In the office, my team and I have a running checklist of things that irritate me in the aesthetics department—things I try to avoid when it comes to how I design a home and analyze the details. Simply put, it's a list of what I consider to be design faux pas that I fiercely avoid. This includes but is not limited to: cold- and blue-hued LED lighting, brown speckled granite, and extra-polished marble. For several reasons, those elements are no-can-dos in my book. I despise them; they make my eyes burn and my stomach hurt. (That's a little harsh, I know, but it's my honest opinion.)

The arches of the built-in cabinetry and shelves were part of the architectural design of this house. We dream up every detail of a home as often as we can to make it feel special.

ABOVE   I designed my own furniture line called Made by Shoppe, and I spent an excruciating amount of time designing pieces with special details, like my signature X-stitch on our Topanga Ottoman and leather buckle on our Mulholland Chairs.

OPPOSITE   Architectural details can make an entire room. In What's the Story, Spanish Glory?, we designed plaster vents with intricate detail in nearly every room of the house to add a subtle and unique nod to Spanish style.

I have always been a detail-oriented person, and that's putting it lightly. I have had strongly worded debates with installers showing me a curtain rod is level when it clearly is not. The fact that it's one centimeter off will keep me up at night. While I can easily find all the things that can go wrong in the project, I will also notice every single detail that's perfect, from a stitch on an ottoman corner to the knobs on a kitchen cabinet to the arches of a doorway to meticulously hand-cut tiles on a vanity. No beautiful detail can cross these eyes without a double thumbs up. I notice it all.

There are a few materials, finishes, and details that I swear by. I am a sucker for oak wood floors, honed marble, patinaed leather, and unlacquered brass—just to name a few—but I take a different approach to these elements every single time. When it comes to designing a new project, I never copy and paste a look I've used before; instead, I've learned to master incorporating details differently each time. To tell you the truth, designing a comfortable home comes down to these raw materials and *how* they are used. Whether it's a wooden button on a pillow, the texture of a linen throw, or the finish on a brass faucet, I stand firm that these details are some of the most important layers to a home.

There is an endless number of ways to pair details, and the pairing doesn't always make sense. Good news: I find that rules are meant to be broken. At the core of my design philosophy, I believe in mixing, mixing, and more mixing! The more you can combine all the things, including even the smallest details, the more you will notice a difference in the end. Maybe you're wondering, "How am I supposed to mix an unlacquered brass faucet and a pendant with a nickel base in the same room?" or "How do two totally different patterns work together?" None of this may make any sense, so I am going to share how I mix it all together in every nook and cranny of a home, and some tips so you can, too.

This master bath is all about simplicity and the mix of a few complementary finishes and materials: unlacquered brass plumbing, bronze finish on the sconces, marble countertops, and reeded oak cabinetry.

TILE SPEAKS IN MOODS
AND ADDS SOMETHING
SUPER SPECIAL TO A
SPACE.

GETTING DOWN
TO BRASS TACKS

When you really start to think about how many decisions you need to make to nail down the details, it can be a bit shocking and mind-boggling. So, let's take this time to break it all down detail by detail.

TILE One tile decision can completely transform the look of a home and, while that may feel overwhelming, it's precisely why I love tile so much. I could drool over the endless options all day before I decide which ones I will actually use—which is what always seems to happen. Picking a tile is arguably even more difficult than choosing a paint color, but, to me, the madness is by far the best part of it all. Tile speaks in moods and adds something super special to a space. Because you have so many choices, you have the opportunity to make your space one of a kind. On top of choosing the actual tiles, of which there are a bajillion colors, shapes, textures, and sizes, you need to figure out the pattern. Will it be subway, herringbone, straight, or diagonal? Because tile also brings in texture, color, and pattern, you have the option to scale back on other elements you might be considering, such as textiles and paint colors. Sometimes the less-is-more approach can really elevate your overall look. After digging through what feels like a million options, you'll land on a combination that feels right to you, and you'll find that it communicates so much about you and your home. At the end of the day, I think tile can speak a lot about your personality.

In the master bath at Bu Round Two, we went with a neutral zellige tile and laid it out in a herringbone pattern, which added texture, movement, and color—three design elements that are a must!

ABOVE   Floor tile is a simple and easy way to add pattern and color, especially to a small room.

OPPOSITE   Here's another use of a neutral zellige tile (see also page 101) in the kitchen of What's the Story, Spanish Glory?, this time laid horizontally in a subway pattern.

LEFT We used a neutral zellige tiles subway-style on the shower walls and hexagonal ones on the shower floor. The colors are cohesive, but the different shapes keep your eyes moving.

CENTER Terra-cotta floor tile in funky shapes and a pink chair rail border break up the white subway tile, creating a delicate mix of pretty and playful in this little girl's bathroom.

OPPOSITE We mixed color and pattern on the floor tile with clean subway tile on the walls to keep the tile theme running throughout this entire home.

We used a bold patterned tile for the kitchen backsplash to add a bit of character in a slightly more traditional kitchen.

WHAT'S THE STORY, SPANISH GLORY?

This original 1920s Spanish-style home located in Pacific Palisades, California, was a two-and-a-half-year project from start to finish. We (my team—an incredible contractor and architect) started working on this from the very beginning with preservation in mind. We knew that extensive work needed to be done, which would include taking the house down to the studs and reworking the less-than-functional floor plan. Our main goals were, as much as possible, to keep the original Spanish detail that made the home unique and to be mindful that anything we added had to complement those gorgeous existing details. From the arches to the plaster vent design to an original stained-glass window to the tile selections, we were not messing around in the unique architectural elements department. In fact, when it came time to photograph this home, we spent the majority of the days shooting every inch. There was so much to capture, and I was so invested in showing off the level of thought and care that went into this house.

One of the most recognizable ways we maintained the Spanish charm was with the architectural materials used throughout. Tile was a big element that really set the stage for not only color, but also the noticeable detail and added interest! Adding various patterns to the stair risers, kitchen backsplash, showers and bathrooms, walls, floors, and the insides of the fireplaces—I cannot think of a place where we didn't incorporate beautiful tile in one way or another. We needed not only to narrow down the tiles we were obsessed with (which took, ooohh, about forever) but also to make sure they complemented our other materials like the colors of the countertops, the tones of the wood, and all the fabrics.

A peek through arched sliding doors into the dining room of What's the Story, Spanish Glory?

ABOVE   The entryway arches perfectly frame the living room, which we layered with several pieces, including my Riviera Sofa from Shoppe Amber Interiors.

OPPOSITE   We filled the entryway with vintage pieces to help complete the warm and neutral color palette of rusts and olive found elsewhere in the home.

LEFT   A close-up of the alter-
nating patterned tile from the
staircase on the previous page.

OPPOSITE   This laundry room
includes loads of storage, a
massive sink, white tile on the
walls with terra-cotta on the
floors. We chose matte black
hardware to pair with the black
countertops and windows.

As I mentioned, tile can be a tricky thing, and especially tricky when you use different kinds in multiple patterns, colors, and shapes in one home. So, how did we make it all work together in this project? It was all about mixing complementary textures, colors, and styles. We were going for a laid-back California-meets-Spanish-hacienda vibe, so we kept the color palette earthy, warm, and muted. All the whites we used in paint and tiles were on the warmer side with hints of cream and beige, though we added a few pops of black and blue. The paint we chose for the entire home was White Heat by Dunn-Edwards, which is one of my all-time fave warm whites. The terra-cotta tiles used on the entryway and laundry room floors were perfectly patinaed to a rusty color that resonates richly. This house was all about the flow of a color story that I wanted to achieve through the smallest of details that would be powerful enough to tie the entire home together.

This kitchen incorporates a simple and clean zellige tile along the perimeter, framing a Spanish-inspired patterned tile for the backsplash.

ABOVE A close-up of the patterned backsplash and Lacanche range.

OPPOSITE A look into the kitchen from the butler's pantry, featuring a custom island and leather-and-iron bar stools.

ABOVE We designed a custom banquette with rich brown leather and hung a vintage piece of art and sconces on the wall to complete the nook.

OPPOSITE This playroom is located upstairs next to the kids' rooms. We wanted to create a space that was playful but still sophisticated, where the kids could practice their ABCs.

A close-up of the living room, layered with vintage furniture, décor, and, of course, tile detail inside the fireplace and on the hearth.

ABOVE The luxuriously layered master bed sits between two windows dressed with custom roman shades.

OPPOSITE We added another reading nook in the master bedroom near the floor-to-ceiling patio doors, which are bordered by custom drapery. We reupholstered a vintage chaise with a neutral and clean fabric to keep the corner feeling bright.

ABOVE   A built-in shelf in the master bedroom, echoing the arch theme seen throughout the entire home.

OPPOSITE   The master sitting room is beyond cozy with a neutral color palette. Once again, we incorporated an arched doorway but this time with double doors. We layered the sofa with pillows and topped off the space with our Chautauqua Bench from Shoppe Amber Interiors, which doubles as an ottoman and coffee table.

HARDWARE The thought of mixing hardware finish options within the same room can seem confusing, especially when you also have to consider the other materials in that room, like countertops, floors, and walls. The most common question I get is "How on earth does it all work together?" Too many finishes can become overwhelming to the eye, so I suggest starting by picking two finishes per room and see how you feel. Once I land on the two hardware finishes per room, I'll layer in other materials and finishes by way of décor. One finish should be your "focal accent," the other should blend into the room a bit more. If you're gun-shy about mixing finishes, there is absolutely nothing wrong with sticking to one hardware finish throughout the room. As I mentioned, you can always add in another finish by way of lighting or other décor.

I am a big fan of unlacquered brass. It ages naturally, an effect commonly referred to as a "living finish": Its exposure to the water, air, or oils on a person's hands changes the appearance. Getting that timeless finish requires some patience—this antiqued look does not occur overnight—but I dig that kind of commitment. In my opinion, it's the most versatile finish; it can be used in both a traditional or a modern application and still work beautifully.

A finish such as a matte black or a chrome can lean a smidge more modern, as theses finishes have almost zero potential for patina. That said, I do understand that unlacquered brass doesn't work for everyone, especially if you don't have the patience to wait for that initially uneven patinaed look to evolve over time. Luckily there are lots of plumbing companies that offer an "antiqued brass" finish straight off the shelf. The brass will arrive looking like it's been aged and will require much less maintenance. Again, always make sure to order samples and compare them with the other elements in the space. A go-to combo for me: unlacquered brass plumbing fixtures with antiqued brass cabinetry hardware. I find that the combo of the two tones works beautifully. Heck, I would even back the decision to add in some black if you wanted!

For the home Canyon Cool, we chose antiqued brass hardware in the kitchen, which is one of my go-tos for a traditional yet modern feel.

ABOVE   Here's another use of antiqued brass, as seen in the master bathroom at What's the Story, Spanish Glory?

OPPOSITE   A simple and can't-go-wrong finish is matte black. We used it in the laundry room at Oh Hi Ojai to add a clean element to this traditional home.

LEFT   This bathroom was for two kiddos, so we made sure we designed cabinetry with tons of storage for their bits and bobs.

CENTER   This mama needed the ultimate chill zone, so we gave her exactly that. A clawfoot tub encircled by the most gorgeous windows and roman shades. Give her a glass of wine and she's set.

OPPOSITE   A simple yet sophisticated guest bath with marble countertops, the prettiest pendants, and, of course, plenty of storage.

THE ART OF THE UPDATE

SOME FIXES HAVE THE POWER TO INSTANTLY CHANGE A ROOM WITHOUT YOU HAVING TO TACKLE A RENOVATION.

- *Refresh the hardware*
  This can be as simple as switching out the knobs of a door or a dresser in a bedroom to changing the towel bar or toilet paper holder in the bathroom.

- *Paint the walls*
  Even if you're not looking to change the whole look of your house, a fresh coat of paint on your walls or cabinets can do wonders.

- *Wallpaper a room*
  Professionally installed wallpaper changes everything, and you can do it as subtly or loudly as your heart desires.

- *Add tile*
  A small-scale tile upgrade, like the backsplash in your kitchen or your shower, is easy enough. Life is way too short to hate your tile!

- *Buy new curtains or shades*
  If you can swing it financially, this is one area where it really pays to hire a professional. The difference between custom drapery and store-bought drapery is apparent, and I think you should always invest in curtains or shades made specifically for your room. I can also promise you that you will never, ever regret having them hemmed to the right length. My rules with drapery are to always mount the curtain rod higher than the window to make the room feel taller, and to extend the drapery rod past the window so the curtain performs properly. When the curtains are open, they should overlap the window trim by only a few inches maximum so they don't block the light streaming in from the window glass. Alternatively, roman shades provide a slightly more refined look than curtains. If the room needs extra oomph, layer both roman shades and drapes.

- *Install pendants, lamps, or sconces*
  Additional lighting can provide a clean, finished, and refined look and is especially welcome in bedrooms when you need a little reading light. A pretty pendant or sconce can be a worthwhile investment. An even quicker fix is to switch out a generic lampshade with a beautiful patterned or textured shade.

For a fix with impact, try adding new lighting, like we did with a trio of ceramic pendants at the home we call Oh Hi Ojai.

ABOVE   Bedside sconces are always good by me. They open up space on your nightstand and add height to the room—a win-win.

OPPOSITE   Pendants will completely change the look of an entire room. At Welcome to LA We Hope You Stay, we chose three matching pendants for the island and a funky pendant over the banquette.

New hardware can elevate any space. In this kitchen, we chose oil-rubbed bronze hardware to pop against the light greigy cabinets.

ABOVE Whether you're trying to make a space a bit more modern or traditional, you'd be surprised at how a light fixture can be the quickest fix.

OPPOSITE Swap out a table lamp for a sconce that adds height and, of course, a cool look to your bedside.

COUNTERTOPS   There are two major things to consider when picking a countertop for the many surfaces of a home: material and aesthetics. Some materials are more practical than others, but some are aesthetically stunning beyond belief, and maybe a little less practical. I genuinely believe that your home should be *lived in*, which means there are going to be spills on the counters and floors that are out of your control. I get asked a million times a day which materials are "worth it," so let's break it down.

Gorgeous natural stones make it into every home I design, in some way or another—almost always in the form of countertops, especially made of Calacatta (a type of marble), Petit Granit (a type of limestone), and Saratoga leathered quartzite (a type of quartzite). They can be dramatic, they can be subtle, and, best of all, they are always one of a kind. When picking your countertops, take into consideration the colors and materials of your floors and cabinetry. Get at least a 2-by-2-inch sample of each piece of stone you are considering and pair it with a sample of the flooring and/or cabinetry. Similar to swatching paint colors to create a color scheme (see page 34), layer the desired materials on top of each other and take a step back to analyze how the materials work together. As with a lot of design based on personal preference, there is technically no wrong combination here; as long as you like what you've put together and it works visually for your space, then go for it.

When it comes to the countertop finish, I always prefer a honed finish— meaning it's more matte than shiny. Honing the material allows it to wear better over time, without it looking polished. And if you read the previous chapter, you'll know that polished countertops have become a big no-no in my book.

Sometimes you don't have to choose: Here we mixed Gris Catalan limestone on the back counter and apron-front sink with the brighter, classic Calacatta marble on the center island.

ABOVE   Gris Catalan limestone brought some edge to this bright and airy Malibu kitchen.

OPPOSITE   We carried pops of black throughout this entire house, and there was no question about it when it came to these Petit Ganit limestone countertops.

ABOVE   This powder room sink at What's the Story, Spanish Glory? got a major upgrade with a Calacatta marble sink: subtle yet stunning.

OPPOSITE   A floating Nero Marquina counter is gorgeous and bold. We wanted it to be the focal point of this powder bathroom, so we paired it with a soft neutral zellige tile.

A MOMENT ON MARBLE   Let's talk specifically about honed marble. It's elegant, it's elevated, and it's simply gorgeous. If you have ever traveled to Europe or visited a very old home, it's likely you have seen marble and other natural materials that have been used for decades. I've incorporated honed marble into a lot of my projects over the years, and I personally want to give all this marble a not-so-subtle time to shine. From floating sinks to kitchen backsplashes to countertops to showers, honed marble makes just about any room a little extra in the most wonderful way. There are so many marble options out there, and I can promise you that I won't stopping using it . . . ever.

Lately I have been loving marble with dramatic veining in golds, greens, and violets. Veining adds so much edge and interest to a room. Your eye immediately goes to it, and then your eye continues to move through it with each unexpected nuance in every slab. A dramatically veined marble can easily become the focal point in a room. Maybe this trend will fade or mark the decade in which the home was designed, but, at the moment, I don't really care. The veining is naturally occurring, and nature isn't a trend, so can it really ever go out of style?

My clients are always scared of ruining their slabs, but just think about the marble bar counters in a French patisserie or the marble outdoor tabletops in an Italian restaurant. What about all the Grecian fountains made out of marble? This material is meant to be used. It's been around forever, and so I try and remind clients, that wine, lemon, and even oil stains will only add to the surface's character. Lighten up and let your space be lived in.

Here's another example of honed Calacatta marble with dramatic veining that contrasts with the stainless with brass details Lacanche range, painted brick wall, and custom white oak cabinetry—a simple yet elevated mix.

ABOVE Talk about a marble moment! We lined this shower at Canyon Cool floor-to-ceiling with a gorgeous slab of honed Calacatta marble and laid even more marble tile on the floor in a herringbone pattern.

OPPOSITE This master bath at Bu Round Two had a few simple materials, and honed Calacatta marble was one of them. We carried it over from the tub to frame the shower.

Honed Calacatta marble with dramatic veining looks extra gorgeous against the greige cabinets at Canyon Cool.

SPACE

AND

FLOW

AT THIS POINT, YOU KNOW MY THOUGHTS ON COLOR THEORY AND ALL THE ITTY-BITTY DETAILS OF A ROOM. NOW, IT'S TIME TO THINK ABOUT THE BIG GUYS. BY THAT I MEAN THE FURNITURE, LIGHTING, RUGS, MIRRORS, ART, AND MORE.

One question I get asked quite frequently is "How on earth do I make my entire home look and feel cohesive while maintaining a good flow from room to room?" Well, let me start by admitting that this is another one of those things that I am no master at but about which I have learned to trust my instincts. Keep in mind that all spaces are different and there is not one way to arrange a room, but I have a few tricks up my sleeve for achieving a great flow and an awesome layout.

A well-designed home will connect aesthetically from room to room. When I'm designing a home, I have a clear process, the CliffsNotes version of which goes a little something like this: I drown myself in mood boards, take a step back to consider the elements, compare room to room, and ask myself, "Does this all look like it belongs in the same house?" If the answer is, "Oh yeah, it vibes real well," then we give ourselves the green light. If the answer is a maybe, then it's back to the drawing board to figure out why a specific piece doesn't work and what would make the space flow better. The goal is to edit out anything that may not feel like a perfect fit and tweak what needs to be adjusted.

This home was all about the cohesiveness and flow. We made sure each room connected in some way, whether it was through color palette or materials.

The common solution to all of this trickery comes down to one simple design technique: layering. No matter what layout you're working with and no matter the bones of your house, achieving good movement throughout a home can be done by layering pieces that tie each room together. You want each space to have its own personality but still feel part of the same home. For example, a living room will most likely contain a sofa, a chair or two, a coffee table, and various accessories. I'll look at this space and make sure it's not too busy or visually crowded—that there are not too many legs on the furniture pieces or too much fabric in one space. I pay attention to the way the pieces of furniture play off one another: If a piece feels very heavy, then I juxtapose something lighter and more delicate to create balance. And I always make sure to create an interesting and synergistic combination of elements.

Once you have this crucial foundation in place, you can focus on furniture arranging, which is basically an advanced game of Tetris. Begin moving the pieces an inch or two that way or a foot or two the other way to allow for traffic throughout the home. Sometimes flipping a pair of chairs from one side of the room to another can make all the difference in a space. There isn't a one-size-fits-all formula, just plenty of trial and error until you finally realize, "Whoa, now *that* is a room that is arranged to perfection." Trust me, once you get there, you'll know that it feels right. The room will flow, you won't feel like a specific piece is jutting out too far, and you'll easily move around the room.

The family room at West Coast Is the Best Coast had that "whoa" moment of a perfectly Tetris'd room. We sourced or designed each piece to fit specifically in the space.

OPEN CONCEPT

Whenever I can, I suggest an open layout in communal spaces, or places where you entertain and congregate the most, like the kitchen, breakfast nook, and living room. I want these spaces to feel inviting and cozy for people to gather; at the same time I want the room's many functions to instantly make it feel bigger. There is nothing wrong with a cozier space, but I like to reserve those intimate rooms for family and not for where you'll entertain guests. One of the most crucial parts of an open concept layout is figuring out how to easily make all the functions one big space flow. Here's how it's done.

FIND YOUR FOCAL POINT   You know when a beautifully designed room makes you say WOW? Chances are your eyes were drawn to one specific thing at first—probably the focal point—the item or element that quite literally draws your attention more than other things in the room. The cool thing is, a focal point can be achieved through pretty much anything in a room: light fixtures, art, rugs, furniture, or a painted or wallpapered wall. So for every space within an open concept layout, determine what that focal point will be and make it eye catching.

BREAK THE BIG SPACE UP INTO MINI ROOMS   Furniture is the best way to help you do that. Section off an area with a sofa, a dining set, a bench, or lounge chairs and make it distinct. That way, the open space won't feel like one big room full of random stuff. Instead, you'll be drawn to this cozy seating over here or that conversation area over there.

At Say No Morrison, we wanted the family room and kitchen to feel like one big communal space, so we chose our Montana Sectional from Shoppe Amber Interiors to help break up the room.

The layout at Black Houses Are the Best Houses was all about the indoor-outdoor flow. This space celebrated true California living, where the sliding doors could be open year-round to enjoy the beautiful outdoors.

Here's another example of an open-concept layout where we used furniture and a large rug to cordon off an intimate gathering space in an otherwise oversized room.

This room is quite large, but we certainly didn't want the furniture to overcrowd the space. We kept the lines clean and modern and used multiple shapes to keep the eye moving around the space.

PROPORTION 101

Proportion and flow go hand in hand. When furniture proportion in a room is off, you'll quickly know there's something weird going on: Bad proportions can restrict movement through the space. Unfortunately, but fortunately, there are no cookie cutter design rules that you must live and breathe by. (I am proof of this!) While I can give you some general guidelines on proportion that work most of the time, you'll really need to give it a whirl and move things around in your own home until it all feels right for you. The ultimate goal to mastering furniture proportion is to make sure you can move freely and comfortably within the space. You want to ensure you can get from point A to point B without having to dodge a stray pouf or bump into a side table. This all comes down to the size, shape, and placement of your furniture.

To figure out how much walking space you really have in a room, grab a measuring tape and make it your friend—but don't sweat it if you're off by a few inches. My general rule of thumb for achieving enough walking space is to leave a minimum of two or three feet between pieces of furniture. If you're only leaving yourself a foot to get by, I hate to say it, but that piece of furniture probably isn't going to work. Trust me, I've had to let go of some beloved pieces because of this. All for the greater good of the space of course.

Once you've mastered spacing and flow, turn your attention back to layering. For furniture, that means you'll want to vary the shapes. The more diverse your pieces of furniture, the more depth and dimension you automatically add to your space. Plus, it keeps things interesting. There is nothing like adding a unique conversation starter!

My general rule of thumb is to keep three feet between your seating and the table, though don't stress if you're a few inches off.

HOW TO PROPERLY UTILIZE A SMALL SPACE This may seem basic, but you would be surprised at how often people don't listen to this one: Less is more, people! I have a hard time listening to my own advice in this department because I can be a hoarder when it comes to pretty pieces. (I mean, it's kind of my job, right? Right. I'll keep telling myself that.) But in this context, "less is more" refers to as few clunky pieces of furniture as possible. Boxy rectangular pieces can make your space feel cramped, so opt for cleaner lines and lighter-looking pieces. And, even if you want additional seating, don't force it if you can't fit it. If it doesn't fit, it doesn't fit. Benches, poufs, or foldaway chairs that you can store are the best seating options in a small area you want to utilize for more than one purpose.

The other key solution to a small space is proper storage. In fact, it's non-negotiable if you're unwilling to let go of everything. (I mean, who is?!) Declutter by storing extra blankets in baskets, stacking books neatly on the coffee table, or displaying knickknacks on shelves. Opt for a furniture piece with drawers or sliding doors that can hide the not-so-cute but must-have things—we all have them and it's a-okay. A little clearing and storing will do wonders for your room. The bottom line for a small space: Only buy what you need. Keep it light and easy. And store, store, store. Only display items that truly make you happy and that have a story or some significance. I guarantee it will make you feel better.

OPPOSITE Our goal was to make this small space as comfy as possible. We chose the Gwynnie Sectional with a small Topanga Ottoman from our shop and closed off the space visually with a vintage armchair.

OVERLEAF Built-in benches in this family room add extra seating without disrupting the room's flow.

PLAYING WITH SHAPES   People are always asking me, "Do I get a round or rectangular table? What's going to work better in the space?" The simple answer is: Mixing different shapes creates interest—and I dig that philosophy. Different shapes help break up a room, so it doesn't feel cookie cutter or geometric. If the process of picking wildly different pieces sounds overwhelming, the good news is that the mix doesn't have to be dramatic. It can easily be just as effective in small doses, especially if you have a more confined space. Try adding a small round side table to a heavily rectangular room, or opt for a cluster of round coffee tables instead of a square or rectangular one.

We chose the round George Dining Table from Shoppe Amber Interiors versus a long rectangular table. Not only was it the more unexpected option, but it also allowed for traffic to flow more easily around the table.

ABOVE AND OPPOSITE   A dining area with enough
banquette seating that every kid could squeeze in if they
wanted to. The banquette had a durable leather cushion,
which was wrapped around the sturdy Ozzie Dining Table from
Shoppe Amber Interiors.

OVERLEAF   This dining banquette at West Coast Is the Best
Coast had a little bit of everything—curves, straight lines,
spheres—a mix that keeps things interesting.

Mixing shapes can be as subtle as a small round table next to a curvy chair in a
room of rectangular pieces. A round vase and stools can do the trick, too!

RUG RULES   I will keep this short and sweet. The bigger the rug, the better. Just kidding! Rugs are the anchor to the room, and I have a very serious obsession with the good ones. At the beginning of every install, I sift through nearly a hundred rugs before choosing the perfect one for each room and hallway of a home. While the colors and materials of a floor covering truly matter, rug success ultimately comes down to a perfect combo of color, pattern, and size. If it's too small, I promise you that it will drive you c-r-a-z-y. Hear me loud and clear on this one, folks: Don't go small because you love the rug and the larger size is out of your budget. I promise that you will find another option that works better; you may have to shop till you drop and hold out for the perfect find.

I'm frequently asked how a rug should fit proportionately in a room, and, as you might know by now, I am not a huge fan of hard and fast rules. That said, I'll give you something to work with:

- *Runners.* Whether it's for the kitchen, bathroom, or hallway, a runner needs to be long enough for the space. When the runner is too short, the room feels big and unfilled. The length of a runner is relative to your space, but if you can leave about two to three feet from the ends before hitting a wall or door, you're in good shape.

This was a long hallway, and thank goodness we were lucky enough to find two similar vintage runners to carry us through the entire stretch!

Here's an example where the back legs of lounge chairs don't fit on the rug. This is totally okay!

- *Area rugs.* Living room rugs should be expansive enough for most of your furniture to sit on top. In many cases, I will find a rug that's large enough for an entire sofa, coffee table, and lounge chairs to fit onto. However, there have also been instances where the back legs of the sofa or lounge chairs do not sit on the rug, and that is okay. You want to know the great news? In my opinion, as long as the front legs are always on the rug, you're in good shape. For the bedroom, make sure the rug is about three feet wider than your bed and at least a tad longer than the width of your side tables. I also aim to get enough rug so that three feet extends from the foot of your bed. The back of the rug doesn't have to touch the front legs of your bedside table, but if it does, make sure it sits beneath the back legs, too. It's an all or nothing situation.

These tidbits all seem simple and kinda obvious to me, but I realize that these "rules" can sound rigid and make design and décor feel intimidating to most people. Luckily, rules are made to be broken, so feel free to take into consideration my thoughts on flow, proportion, shapes, and sizes, but be sure to apply your own thoughts and ideas. Do what works best for you and you'll quickly master your space—and get a handle on this whole design thing real fast.

ABOVE   Dining room chairs should all comfortably fit on the rug so no one trips when getting up or sitting down.

OPPOSITE   This big ol' vintage rug fit just right in this room, leaving a bit of space between the rug and the front of the nightstand.

THE

ART

OF

STYLING

THE YEAR 2011 WAS A BIG ONE FOR ME. THOSE WERE MY EARLY BLOGGING DAYS, AND I WAS TRYING TO GET MY DESIGN STUDIO OFF THE GROUND. ANY CHANCE I COULD GET, I WOULD GO TO EVERY FLEA MARKET, GARAGE SALE, AND THRIFT STORE NEARBY TO PURCHASE THINGS FOR MYSELF AND MY CLIENTS.

Before I knew it, all of those shopping trips added up to quite the collection of pillows, textiles, rugs, and other finds. As I mentioned, I am inherently a bit of a hoarder (thanks Dad and Papa), so I was buying a few more treasures than I really needed, and the overflow was getting a little ridiculous. My garage could have been featured in an episode of *Hoarders*. At least the stuff was pretty!

Owning this finders-keepers mentality got me really excited about all the one-of-a-kind pieces out there. Someone's trash was literally my new treasure. I could fix up my collectibles, give them a little cleaning, and they would be the perfect décor items in my own home and the homes I was designing. I quickly realized that this step in my design process was crucial to my signature look. I felt like I had developed a true design aesthetic, one that seemed unique enough to share.

Styling and layering brings a room to life. Every piece I use to fill a room tells a story of a time and place that's special to the people who live there.

LAYERING AND STYLING
WILL MAKE YOUR HOME
STAND APART FROM
THE REST.

I always try to add vintage finds from my travels and
obsessive research.

There are definitely parts of the entire design process that I favor more than
others, and I can say with certainty that nothing brings me more joy than adding
those final touches to a home, especially when it's one that I have worked on for
years. Styling a home is the equivalent of tying a ribbon on a gift. You get the
idea—it's the final step. It's the moment when you can bring it all together and, for
me, that happens just before I hand my baby over to the clients. Up to this point
in the book, we've walked through some of the bigger, distinct choices you need
to make—all of which are critical to the look and feel you are ultimately trying
to create. But layering and styling all the little things—that is the secret sauce to
making your home stand apart from the rest.

So here's where I get giddy. It's the time in the entire process when you can
make all those disparate styles and design eras of your pieces come together in a

specific way. I admit, I will go to great lengths to achieve the perfect look, scouring the world seeking the most vintage items I can possibly find. I am a crazy lady and will fight someone at a market if I really want that piece of art—whatever I have to do to decorate a home to perfection. It ain't easy being this obsessed with interior design, but it sure is worth it in the end.

Look, the finished product is what matters. What I have already mentioned when it comes to the intricate details, space, and flow, I will mention again when it comes to styling. The art of mixing and layering is the key ingredient in how it is all done. That is my ultimate design belief, and I am going to talk you through exactly what I mean.

There are several elements that come into play once you begin mixing and layering different fabrics, textiles, and textures. It's time to take into consideration how curtains will look against a paint color or wallpaper, or how seven pillows will look on a couch with a throw or two. All of what I am about to dive into can be hard to articulate, but trust me and try to stay with me, as this step makes all the difference in your home. Let's do it together, shall we?

The more layers the better. Mixing colors, textures, and patterns is what it's all about.

ABOVE   The family room at West Coast Is the Best Coast brings together all my favorite elements: vintage pieces mix with new items—and there are patterns, solids, and textures galore.

OPPOSITE   A vignette of vintage in a cozy corner of the same family room.

Go as crazy as you want with all the patterns, but keep the colors and tones in line to make it work.

MIXING PATTERNS AND TEXTURES

It bears repeating that few things get me more excited than talking patterns and textures, and how they can coexist in a living space. It's always been one of my preferred parts of the design process, and I don't think that will ever change. There is a fine line of finding the perfect balance between too little and too much when it comes to mixing patterns and textures, though. Truth is, I find the generic rules of this to be boring. For instance, some folks will tell you not to put pattern on pattern. What on earth are they even talking about? That is pure blasphemy and doesn't make any sense to me. My friends, it is *ALL* about patterns on patterns on textures on more patterns. When done right—like choosing the right tile, wallpaper, or paint—layering the right patterns with one another will pull your space together and make all your wildest dreams come true. All right, maybe I'm exaggerating, but I am passionate about this part of the process, okay?

Ultimately, your color palette will determine the overall schematic in your décor, and you first need to identify that scheme, the process for which I walked you through in "The Power of Color" (page 15). Mixing patterns in a space comes down to finding prints in the same or complementary color tones. Using similar color tones in different ways throughout the room helps make it easier to nail the pattern-on-pattern look. One of the easiest ways to figure out if a pattern will mesh well with another pattern is to lay all the fabrics you're considering next to each other and on top of each other. Give it the old step-back-and-analyze-it-together trick we keep talking about. If the tones are clashing, try another pattern. Repeat until the tones and patterns vibe for you.

ABOVE   Some of my favorite textiles to layer are kantha quilts, which originate from the Bengali tradition of recycling cotton saris into quilts. The intricate designs are unique, colorful, and happy.

OPPOSITE   A pulled-back view of the family room at Bu Round Two, where we applied layers of pillows, throws, patterns, and more.

ABOVE   While these several layers of subtle patterns are all different, they're cohesive in color and style.

OPPOSITE   The floors get overlooked when it comes to considering pattern, and here's a perfect example of it done right. We placed a vintage rug over a herringbone-patterned brick floor for a happy pairing.

WEST COAST IS THE BEST COAST

When I was designing the little girl's room in a client's home, I pulled in about a hundred different patterns on just about every layer possible within the space. From curtains to wallpaper to upholstery—to pillows, rugs, and throws—I didn't leave anything out. I took it a step further by layering the patterns on top of one another, giving the room a bit of something extra. For example, I layered a patterned pillow on a very different patterned upholstered chair. I placed a patterned rug on the floor, while picking a completely different patterned wallpaper for the ceiling. I knew I wanted this room to be bright, full of energy, and sweet at the same time—and if I haven't made it obvious yet, our plan was to do this with pattern. At the beginning of the décor and layering process, we identified a very distinct color palette of pinks and blacks and whites. Then, to break up some of the patterns and layers ever so slightly, I incorporated a few anchoring pieces—like a solid wood dresser and desk, a solid-colored blanket, and a woven basket—that played well with all the texture. The focal point of this room was undoubtedly the patterned wallpaper on the ceiling. Without the wallpapered ceiling, this would have been very, very different. I wanted this space to make a statement, and the extra oomph from up top was exactly how I envisioned pattern playing well in this space.

Now *this* is what I call mixing patterns! We went bold with printed wallpaper on the ceilings, floral upholstery, and a vintage kantha throw. Pattern adorns absolutely everything, but the pieces all tie together with a cohesive color palette.

MIXING OLD AND NEW   Using vintage pieces is one of the most effective ways to mix and layer traditional and modern elements in a home. Whether the vintage pieces come in the form of textile, furniture, or smaller décor, old finds immediately add charm, personality, and warmth to a space in a way that other elements, like color, can't achieve. Yes, color can do incredible things, but it can't tell a story like a decades-old dresser or table can. Also, the fact that no one else will have the same exact piece is pretty rad.

I tend to upset a lot of folks when I tell them a piece is one-of-a-kind. Trust me, I wish there were another one lying around, too. Finding old pieces with good bones is not an easy feat. I spend a lot of time, and I mean *a lot*, scouring for vintage. This is where I try to tell you to take the slow and steady approach to finding the perfect piece, and you might already guess that I can barely listen to my own advice here. If you know exactly where the piece is going, I definitely suggest buying it, because finding good vintage is a game of patience, and I get tested on this all the time. Don't let it be the one that got away.

Who says you can't convert a vintage dresser into a kitchen island?

In any given room I design, there is always a decent amount of vintage. It can be a chair reupholstered in a beautiful new fabric, a pillow made from a textile I picked up in Provence, a dining table I stumbled across in upstate New York, or a simple ceramic bowl I found in the fields of Round Top, Texas. I incorporate these irreplaceable finds into every single room. The result: a space that feels a little homier and a lot more special—two fundamentals that are enough for me to continue obsessing over my next vintage find.

ABOVE   The hallway to the wine cellar of Bu Round Two, where an old vibe was just the feel we were going for.

OPPOSITE   The living room in Bu Round Two features special antiques I specifically found for this home—from the Bruno Mathsson midcentury leather chair to a hundred-year-old apothecary cabinet to reupholstered shearling club chairs. I also added a pair of Sage Stools from Shoppe Amber Interiors.

The dining room of Bu Round Two, where at every turn something old mingles with something new.

HOW TO VINTAGE

In my design career, I have probably used, oh say, a million and one vintage pieces in some way, shape, or form. That's just a ballpark though. For one home, I might pick and choose a couple of larger pieces, like furniture, and then some smaller vintage items, like vases and bowls, to methodically sprinkle throughout the home. When it comes to old pieces, remember that you are not curating a museum collection. You are simply incorporating a little history here and there to create the perfect mix of vintage and new pieces within your home. Too much vintage can quickly give a space grandma vibes, so let me share the lowdown on how to mix old and new the right way.

A few things to consider while you shop for vintage:

QUALITY   This is potentially the most important tip of all the tips I am about to list. Ask yourself these questions before purchasing a vintage piece: Is the piece sturdy? Are there stains that can't be fixed with a fresh coat of paint or some new fabric? Is the wood cracking? There are several ways to bring a piece back to life, but if the core of the item is severely damaged, you may need to let it go. I know that ain't easy, but you will thank me later; otherwise, you'll be wasting your hard-earned cash.

TIME INVESTMENT   If the piece checks off the quality box, it may require a bit of fine-tuning once you bring it home. Be realistic about the extra money, time, and research that it might cost you to bring it back to life. Also, save yourself the headache and extra research by asking the vintage dealer if they can recommend a good repairman (unless you're shopping far from home, of course). You may need to do some vendor research on your own here.

BE OPEN-MINDED   One of the thrills of vintage shopping is not knowing what you might find. Of course, go in with the general idea of what you want, but chances are that you will find something a little more unexpected than what you originally had in mind. Often it's better than what you were looking for, and that's the best feeling in the world.

BE PATIENT   I mentioned this earlier, but finding vintage pieces is hard— very hard. Don't settle if you're not in love, because there may not be a return policy. And don't forget to ask yourself, "Does it *actually* fit the space?" Shop with your floor plan and measurements in hand; you'll need them.

ABOVE   Note to self! Not all vintage vases can hold water, so be sure to double-check before you fill it with water and end up with a watermark on your furniture.

OPPOSITE   These vintage stools for the master bedroom at West Coast Is the Best Coast were sturdy and functional. I wouldn't have picked them if they weren't, especially in a room where space is precious and every piece gets used.

ABOVE   When shopping at flea markets, be on the lookout for small knick-knacks, like bowls and vases, that you can add to your space. You don't always have to put the piece to use—being decorative is enough excuse for you to bring it home.

OPPOSITE   We wanted to add a little extra character to this new and relatively traditional mudroom. Voilà: a spruced-up vintage dresser and decorative accessories did the trick.

LEFT Vintage can come in all shapes, sizes, and functions! This limestone sink and mirror in the powder room at Bu Round Two made the room entirely.

CENTER Another vintage mirror I found in Texas that worked perfectly in the guest bath at Bu Round Two.

OPPOSITE Here's a more creative way to repurpose an antique. We turned this dresser into a bathroom vanity by replacing the top and adding a sink and plumbing.

MORE STYLING SECRETS

The following pages capture my all-time favorite ideas for finishing a room—including pillows, shelves, and bed layers. Then, because kitchens, living rooms, and master bedrooms always get all the attention, let's dive into a few often overlooked rooms that pay dividends when you focus on amping up the details.

PILLOWS   My serious obsession with textiles includes pillows. I truly think they can make or break a room. One wrong pillow and it all goes downhill. I am kind of sort of kidding, but mostly one hundred percent serious. Long before I opened my first brick-and-mortar store, Shoppe Amber Interiors in Calabasas, California, there was a time in which I was selling pillows via Instagram from fabrics I sourced and sewed myself, along with other décor I found from treasure hunting on trips and at flea markets. This was right about the time when Instagram first launched, or at least when I first started paying attention to it, so this was all new territory, and I had no idea what I was doing. People were very into my pillows, though, and the goods were selling like hotcakes. My home garage was overflowing with pillows, and I kind of loved it, but I was also feeling suffocated at the same time. Those pillows and treasure-hunted items were, in a way, the beginning of my career.

Over the years, I have learned a lot about the history of textiles, how they are made, where they are sourced, and how they can become myriad home décor items that adorn our sofas and beds. As you know, pillows come in all sorts of shapes, sizes, color, fabrics, and patterns. Let me break down the different types and the factors that come into play when you are choosing pillows for a specific room.

Don't shy away from layering on the pillows; doing so will complete any and all rooms. If you can sit on it, it probably needs a pillow or two!

- *Basic.* This is probably one of my most frequently used pillow types. Don't let the term "basic" fool you though, because these beauties are anything but! They often have simple patterns or stripes and can be found in any color. In the designer world, we often refer to the basics as our foundation pieces typically used as the backdrop to the rest of your collection. Think vintage linen, one-of-a-kind "grain sacks," a patternless African mud cloth. Nothing too jarring or bold is usually my go-to for the foundational layer.

- *Embroidered.* You'll see plenty of these particular vintage fabrics in homes I've designed and in my stores; they are typically sourced from Asia and are remnants of old clothing, like gowns, skirts, and jackets. In most cases, they have gorgeous, intricate stitching and can be found in a range of colors and also in minimalist palettes.

- *Ikat and batik.* These pillows are made with resist-dying techniques. The ikat process happens when the thread is dyed before it's handwoven into a pattern, whereas in the batik process the resist is applied to the final cloth, not to the thread.

- *Indigos.* An Amber Interiors staple for years, this textile is made from an organic compound and natural dye found in plants. The process to incorporate them into textiles can involve several techniques such as twisting, wrapping, or even stitching. The deep rich hue of blue can really make a huge statement.

A few examples of how I mix pillows, combining subtle patterns, textures, colors, and sizes.

IN MY ROOMS, YOU WILL
RARELY SEE THE SAME
TWO PILLOWS MIRRORED
ON BOTH SIDES OF A SOFA.

HOW TO CREATE THE PERFECT PILLOW COMBO   Pulling together pillows is my kind of therapy. When the mix is right, it has the power to finish the entire room and make all feel right with the world. When I'm picking pillows for a space—be it a sofa, bed, bench, or nook—I consider quite a few factors. First of all, I don't like things to be perfectly symmetrical or expected. I want to keep the eye interested while it's scanning a space. In my rooms, you will rarely see the same two pillows mirrored perfectly on both sides of a sofa, but I always keep the color story consistent. So, when I'm deciding on pillows, I look for different variations and textile types (see page 217), and I always consider the color palette, patterns, and textures (see page 193).

Keep it simple and go with what you know and love. Start by choosing a favorite pillow and giving it a job! Either use it as the foundation or anchoring piece if it's more minimal, or as the accent piece if it has a fun pattern or color—and then continue to build from there. The anchor piece is typically the largest pillow in the back; the rest vary in width and height and sit in front of the anchor. When picking the second layer of pillows, choose another pillow or two that balance the anchor yet differ in texture, size, and color. The last layer, or accent pillow, should be the smallest of the bunch to top off your combo and potentially pack a punch in either color or pattern. The most important takeaway with pillow collections is to make sure the color tones work together. If the color palette is cohesive, then the patterns should mix perfectly.

Warm and neutral textured pillows fill a deep-seated sofa in the master sitting room of What's the Story, Spanish Glory?

ABOVE   We used pillows and throws to add much-needed punches of color, texture, and pattern in this neutral-hued room.

OPPOSITE   We pulled in the rusts and blues from the kitchen to the pillows. And, of course, every cozy sofa needs a big chunky blanket to curl up with.

#**SHELFIE**   Whether it's a nook within a cabinet or a floor-to-ceiling library, I take styling shelves very seriously. Shelves can house a collection of several things, but the arrangement should look intentional, not jumbled. The items on a shelf should display beautiful memories and mementos that speak to you. Notice my use of the word "beautiful" here, because it's an important one. Ahem, keep that bizarre gift you got from Aunt Judy in storage, okay? We're looking for the pieces in your home that you're proud of and want everyone to casually see so that you can easily say "Oh? That ol' thing?" and secretly feel proud that you just became cooler in the eyes of whoever just saw it. Fine, maybe that's a shallow reason why your shelves should be well styled, but they are a great place to up your décor game and show off your most prized possessions.

Most important, a shelf should feel clean and organized. It should never look cluttered or give you anxiety. When a shelf is fully styled, you should take a step back and say to yourself, "That's a damn good-looking shelfie." Let's walk through a few key tips and tricks to get you started.

A shelfie in the dining room of Bu Round Two, complete with cookbooks, glassware, art, and vintage décor.

1 *Pick the items.* Depending on the room, choose items that are most representative of that space. For example, limit the kitchen shelfie to mainly tabletop items and the living room shelfie to books, artwork, mementos, and a family photo or two. The items need to make sense and belong. Also, keep in mind that shelves can house so much more than just books, so be creative here. (I would call it a bookshelf if that's what it was!) Pro tip: Do not include anything smaller than the size of an apple, unless the items are in groupings. Such items on their own are too small and will clutter the look.

2 *Start placing items on the shelf.* When I look at a shelf, I want to keep the eye moving around easily. Make sure to change it up: Place books both vertically and horizontally or use a stack of books as a bookend. Then combine a bunch of interesting touches like vintage pieces or a plant. More often than not, I will place a ceramic bowl or vessel on top of a stack of books to add height. I also love to lean a vintage piece of art behind the styled items to fill space and to add height and dimension.

3 *Step back and observe.* This is something you should be doing several times while you're pulling your shelf together. It's okay if it takes a long time—it should. Once you have a good base layer of things on the shelves, it's time to think about color theory again. Check to see if an anchor color in one piece is visible elsewhere on the shelf. I call this the "ping-pong effect": I want your eye to bounce around the shelf as you notice pops of the same color in a few places. If you use a black vase on top of a stack of books, make sure you add another pop of black a couple of shelves down.

4 *Don't overdo it.* Chances are, you will have a lot you want to showcase and get on that shelf. But one of the biggest mistakes I often see is too much stuff, resulting in clutter. When you look at the shelfie, you should feel calm and organized. If those two words don't come to mind when you step back and observe, keep editing down. You'll get there. Remember, you can always change things out. Nothing is permanent.

LEFT Stack books both horizontally and vertically to add height and to keep the eye moving across the space.

RIGHT Kitchen shelfies should be practical. Display the bowls and plates you use daily on the shelves and start stacking!

ABOVE Shelfies should also incorporate different materials and textures. Here we included brass, handmade ceramics, glasses, and a textured vintage vase.

OPPOSITE If you have tall ceilings, add height to the top shelf, like we did here with a vintage cutting board and candlestick holders.

PLENTY MORE

MINA STONE   COOKING FOR ARTISTS

LEFT   Mixing and layering is not just for pillows and throws. Combining different textures (roughhewn wood, dented vintage metal objects, handmade pottery, and plants) and stacking objects in different ways will do the trick.

CENTER   Here's a clean and not overly styled shelf. It's a bar, after all, so things are probably going to get busy around there!

OPPOSITE   A shelfie in the library of Bu Round Two that shows off our clients' treasured mementos. We layered in their favorite books, vintage objects, and art.

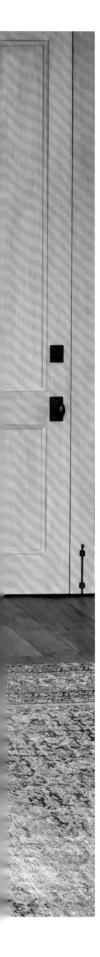

I WILL MAKE AND REMAKE
A BED UNTIL THE LAYERS
ARE RIGHT.

BED LAYERS   When I was a kid, my mom did not give me the option to leave the house until my bed was made. Turns out, that rule really stuck with me, because my daughter, Gwyneth, is certainly not allowed to leave the house until her bed is made either. Over the years, I have become *quite* the diligent bedmaker. It's a rule that I'm glad my mom instilled in me, because look at me now: It has fully carried into my job. I will make and remake a bed until the layers are right, the corners are tucked in properly (or sometimes let out!), and the wrinkles are smoothed. No matter if I'm in my own home, a hotel, or leaving a client's home after an install, I've got to leave the house knowing each bed is made to perfection. I get asked time and time again, how do you style a bed? Let's break it down, okay?

The master bedroom at Bu Round Two, where we kept the
layers simple and warm.

- *Start with sheets.* Seems obvious, but this can be a difficult part of the process. While there are a lot of options out there, I feel boring might be better when choosing sheets. There is nothing wrong with crisp white cotton bedding. I am not even going to beat around the bush on this one, because it's the real truth. I am one hundred percent a sucker for cotton percale sheets, and white or ivory is never a wrong choice. If color is your jam, try to keep it neutral. We want to layer, so anything too bold will make this job tough. To keep the bed ensemble clean looking, don't forget to tuck in the sheets carefully.

- *Choose a duvet cover.* I am constantly asked if the sheets need to match the duvet cover. The answer is no! Mix 'em all you want, but stay in the same color story, because the next step is all about introducing additional colors and textures with throws, quilts, blankets, and pillows.

- *Pick a couple of throws, quilts, or blankets.* Not only is this the obvious best way to add warmth to your bed, but it instantly gives you another layer for adding color, texture, pattern—or all the above. The most important thing here is to make sure you find something that goes with your color story. (Head back to pages 214 to 217 for a refresh!) Don't be afraid of pattern here— I am a sucker for a patterned quilt over a bed!

- *Layer on the pillows.* This is the icing on the cake. I walked you through my basics on pillow combos a few pages back (see page 218), so apply them. One thing you can do to add a layer of color or pattern is to use for your main sleeping pillows pillowcases that are different from the ones that came with the set of sheets. Like I have said before, go ahead and break the rules.

On the bed of this master bedroom, we brought in multiple throws in different textures and several pillows. Then we added another layer of gorgeous textiles in the way of curtains and roman shades.

LEFT   At the home I call Double Thumbs Up, we chose a simple layer with tons of texture, a crisp, white duvet cover, and punches of black in the pillow to add some edge.

CENTER   An example of my standard for layering pillows: first add a basic foundational layer, then throw in an embroidered pillow, and top it off with something indigo.

OPPOSITE   Never underestimate the power of texture in a bedroom.

There's no such thing
as too many patterns,
especially when they're
subtle; layering them gives
a room that extra oomph.

Everywhere you look in this room, a comfortable seat awaits thanks to an abundance of warm throws and textured pillows.

WHEN CHOOSING DÉCOR
FOR YOUR ENTRYWAY, YOU
ARE GOING TO WANT TO
FOCUS ON HOW YOU WILL
USE THIS SPACE.

ENTRYWAYS   This is the space where you can make your first impression. I like to save the entryways for a stunning piece of art, an insanely gorgeous light fixture, or a knockout rug and console table moment. When choosing décor for your entryway, you are going to want to focus on how you will use this space. Will it be your main entry for guests and your family? If so, try to find a piece of furniture that will handle all of your needs while being aesthetically pleasing as well. If you need storage, look for an unexpected console with hidden compartments, or install hooks for hanging your pretty hats and keys. If items tend to collect in this space, invest in some decorative baskets to keep your stuff from looking cluttered and crazy.

The most grandiose yet welcoming entryway from Bu Round Two. We mixed modern and traditional elements that make you feel the "wow" but also give you that familiar feeling of being home.

ABOVE   An arched door with stained glass immediately communicates warm California-meets-Spanish vibes as soon as you step onto the terra-cotta floors.

OPPOSITE   This traditional entryway from West Coast Is the Best Coast features my Anderson Console table—ideal for storing keys and keeping other on-the-go items within reach.

A MOMENT ON MUDROOMS I didn't have a mudroom growing up in Malibu, California, maybe because my parents, like most Californians, didn't quite see the need for one with our warm climate. As a kid, I had always dreamed of schlepping in a sled or a pile of firewood that I could drop at the door, but I dragged in pounds of sand and seashells from the beach instead. So, when I got to designing homes on the East Coast and beyond, I channeled my lifelong mudroom-making dreams. A mudroom should be practical. After all, it's a place to dump your dirty stuff, kick off your shoes, and make a mess. There needs to be a place to hang your coat or towels, storage for boots, a place to sit and get your shoes on—you know, the basics. It's also important to think about materials, such as flooring. You need to choose a material that will be easy to clean and is not too precious. Brick or some kind of stone is always a good move.

This Northern California mudroom is pretty, simple, and functional with herringbone-patterned floors, tons of storage, and a farmhouse sink—in short, a mudroom made right.

CONNECTICUT CUTIE

This design was for a family of seven—two parents, four young kids, and one Bowie (the Golden Retriever)—who needed a big and practical mudroom for kiddos and the dog to plow through after playing in the nearby snowy fields. So we widened the hallway significantly to let the room breathe and to create enough space for six humans and a Golden Retriever to roam. Next up, we added wall paneling and new cabinetry for all the storage we could possibly incorporate. Let's all take a moment to remember that kids are not tidy or organized whatsoever, so I wanted to design something that was easy and made sense to the kids when they entered the home. When it came to flooring, we salvaged what we could from the original brick floors and funked it up by laying the bricks in a herringbone pattern, which complemented the traditional wall paneling and ultimately gave this room a cool, upscale farmhouse vibe. File this under "I'm moving to Connecticut to justify having a mudroom like this."

The mudroom with the original brick floors re-laid in a new pattern.

KIDS' SPACES I've been lucky enough to work with lots of families with lots of kiddos, and I must admit: Designing their rooms is really gratifying. Remember my mindset as a kid (see page 16)? I took my pink bedroom design very seriously. So, lucky for my clients' kids, their rooms usually get extra attention, because my kid-self is still alive and pretty darn obsessed with design stuff. I always seem to end up with a happy kid client.

For me, a kid's space should be *f-u-n*. It should be a place for kids to be inspired, feel safe, and make awesome memories. From a design perspective, it's the perfect time to incorporate exciting patterns and colors that I wouldn't necessarily consider for other rooms. This can be done by way of wallpaper, pillows, blankets, upholstered furniture—you name it. Most of the time, I'll mix all of those elements together. The result? A creative and entertaining space.

A kid's room should also be functional. If you are like me and have a kiddo, you know the terror of instant clutter. To minimize the chaos, I design with ample storage in mind. From drawers, cubbies, shelves, and cabinets to baskets, you can never have too much of *that* in a kid's room. What's my general rule of thumb when designing and decorating a kid's room? Ask the kid! Get their opinion and put your spin on it. There's nothing better than seeing a smile on a kid's face when they feel like they've been heard. Even if it's asking them what their favorite color is—a little input goes a long way.

This was a tall and narrow room, so we decided a bunk bed would be the perfect design solution. We went with white oak as the main material to flow the design with the rest of Bu Round Two.

One of my fave kid's rooms I recently designed was the custom bunk bedroom at Bu Round Two. The room was narrow but had really high ceilings, so we opted for a bunk bed to fully maximize the space. Not to mention that the bottom queen bed and top twin bed would make for an awesome tween's room. When it came to choosing materials, it was a no-brainer to go with natural white oak, as it was already the running theme throughout the rest of the house. (Side note: Carrying similar materials throughout a home is key! Flip back to It's All in the Details, pages 90 to 103, for a deeper dive.) The major design challenge in this room was that we didn't want the bunk bed to feel dark and cave-like, as so many bunk beds can feel. So, we designed slatted wood pieces at the back of the bookshelf that was closest to the window to allow natural light to flow into the bottom bunk. This bed is cool, it's practical, and it makes me want to be a kid all over again.

We opted for slatted wood pieces at one end of the bed so the bottom bunk could still get some natural light flowing in, without it feeling cave-like, which always tends to be a design flaw with bunk beds.

This is a cool room for a cool kid. We wanted this room
to last through the teenage years—just take out the toy
truck and suddenly it's all grown up.

We filled this naturally bright room with colorful patterns.
The window seating nook would be exactly where I'd spend
my tween years, curled up, reading a book.

One of my all-time-favorite bunk rooms, with layers
of the prettiest pillows and throws that kids will never
grow out of. To maximize playing room, we chose to
build bunk beds and create more floor space.

ABCDE
FGHIJ
KLMNO
PQRST
UVWXY
Z

ABOVE   A girls' bath doesn't have to be all-pink; keep it neutral to last through those teenage years.

OPPOSITE   This kids' bath in Malibu had a nautical vibe with some LA cool. Funky pendants and a piece of art I found antiquing mixed with dark elements made this a room that will last for years to come.

A WORD ON WORKSPACES　As an entrepreneur, I fully understand the need for an inspiring and productive workspace. It needs to feel energetic yet calm. Bright but not distracting. You need privacy, but there should be room for collaboration. I take all of these elements into consideration when I'm designing my own workspaces, as well as a client's. On top of all of these things, I want to make sure the space feels homey but not *so* comfortable that you might fall asleep on the job. Above all else, the space needs to fuel creativity and efficiency.

For starters, find yourself a comfortable chair and desk. If you have a lot of *things*, look for a desk with drawers that optimize space and provide storage solutions. If I've learned anything over the years, it's that a comfy chair will keep you productive. Second, keep the overall space simple yet inviting. Your workspace should be as clutter-free as possible, but I know how hard that can be in an office with papers and binders and other such items. This is where coming up with storage solutions becomes important. If you have cabinets, even better, but don't just cram all of your stuff all into cabinets and drawers; keep your work and supplies organized even when they're stored away. If you need to create storage, there are so many pretty bins, folders, trays, and boxes available these days that can store it all. I am a personal fan of a #shelfie in the office, too (page 229). It's a great way to showcase books, awards, or mementos that inspire you. Light, bright, and pristine are the name of the game.

A few secrets to a productive WFH space: keep your desk uncluttered and situate it in a naturally lit room.

BU ROUND TWO

This Malibu project was special. Not only because it was perfectly situated on an acre-and-a-half beachside property surrounded by an array of mature orange, avocado, lemon, and lime trees, but also because the clients who owned the property could not have been dreamier to work with. The unique combination of amazing people and a stunningly setting made the project a winner from the start.

This particular home was quite the mental undertaking. Literally every single inch of architectural detail and décor in the home was chosen with obsessive attention to detail. From picking the paint to choosing the tile, the countertops, and the floor stain . . . not one decision was made without careful thought and consideration. I had to look at each material chosen in relation to how it would affect every other decorative element in the house, which was no easy task in a 6,000-plus square foot home. The goal was to strike the perfect balance of mixing numerous materials and maintaining the overall aesthetic from room to room. When it all finally came together, it was truly my version of perfection.

Before we got our hands on this home, the existing materials, while elegant, felt dark and a little heavier than what my clients were looking for. Our goal was to design a home that would make you feel like you were still in California, but possibly in a fabulous Belgian farmhouse, too. We needed to lighten up the entire space, add in some architectural arches and hand-hewn beams, replace all the cabinetry, redo all the plumbing and fireplaces, change the flooring, and paint every surface. It was quite the undertaking, but one I gladly took on.

We custom-designed hutches to frame this entire room, with the Simeon Dining Table from Shoppe Amber Interiors and classic Pierre Jeanneret teak-and-cane chairs situated in front of the fireplace.

RIGHT   We designed this entryway to feel grandiose yet welcoming.

OPPOSITE   Although the living room was sizable and had tall ceilings, it ended up being quite the cozy room, full of earthy materials and tones with punches of rust and camel. We wanted this to be a place where the homeowners could curl up on the sofa and chill.

OVERLEAF   This kitchen is a mix of natural materials and earthy tones. We chose reclaimed French limestone floors, designed custom white oak cabinetry, and sourced both Calacatta marble and Gris Catalan limestone countertops—all of which achieves that "been there forever" rustic farmhouse vibe.

To start, we chose for the walls a plaster finish called Roman Clay by Portola Paints. This smooth but textured look helped add a visual layer that gave the home a little bit of drama in the best way possible. The ceilings were high—like really, really high—and I wanted the walls to feel like an interesting enough element that you took notice when stepping into each room. The texture would help add depth to the space and keep it from feeling like just another white-painted room. Not like I have anything against that, but, still, I wanted it to WOW! We kept the tone of the plaster on the warmer side and chose a few different complementary colors for various rooms. The beauty of the texture is that your eye could see the difference in tone, but the texture and subtle variation in color made the transition seamless and tied all the rooms together.

When it came to the floors, we were already lucky enough to be working with a beautiful existing material. The previous owners had installed vintage imported European solid oak plank custom milled floors in varying widths and lengths. These types of floors are almost impossible to come by anymore, so getting to work with such a stunning material was a score. Unfortunately, we inherited them with a dark espresso, slightly sun-faded stain on them. While gorgeous in theory, it was bringing the whole vibe of the space down a bit—and it had to go!

As I said, lightening up the entire space was the name of the game, so we stripped the finish and re-stained all the flooring with a custom-mixed white with honey-toned oak stain. Getting these floors back to their original glory and then trying to maintain the color proved difficult, but we worked with a very skilled contractor, Jones Group Malibu, who achieved the unachievable. However, when it came time to tackle the kitchen floor, I decided I wanted it to feel a little more rustic and juxtapose the more modern cabinetry we designed. Much to our budget's dismay, we ended up sourcing a reclaimed French limestone floor from Exquisite Surfaces, which gave the home a big dose of rustic farmhouse charm without making it feel too contrived. To match the rest of the home's lived-in, warm and rustic vibes, we chose unlacquered brass plumbing, used reclaimed limestone wall-mounted sinks in the powder rooms, and topped our cabinetry with Gris Catalan limestone, Petit Granit, and honed Calacatta marble.

The flooring we chose for the kitchen was reclaimed French limestone, which added so much character and lent the home a rustic and charming yet elevated look.

LEFT   We designed a handwoven wicker banquette with a leather cushion, which wraps around the dining table. We couldn't find a table we loved for this space, so we specifically designed this pedestal base table, which we named the Morgan Dining Table and is now part of my furniture line.

CENTER   We designed a solid oak cabinet with a v-groove detail to complement the rustic yet modern European style of the rest of this kitchen.

OPPOSITE   This unlacquered brass faucet by Waterworks is a modern and timeless pairing with the Calacatta marble.

To create a super chill family room, you have to focus on the layers. We mixed in all sorts of different materials and textures but kept everything soft and cozy.

As I mentioned, tailoring every inch of this home was seemingly the only way to go. When we first walked onto this property months before we began construction, I knew it was too special not to. Customizing the cabinetry throughout the entire home was a big detail that I needed to get right. It had to feel unique and a departure from the standard ol' cabinets we see all the time. It also, somehow, had to be different enough from room to room, while keeping the overall aesthetic flowing.

We decided to use solid white oak as the main material on nearly all the cabinets throughout the home. We used unique details to differentiate the cabinets from space to space, but we made sure each room ended up speaking to the next. In "her" master bathroom, it was all about the simplicity in the materials. The reeded oak cabinetry detail, the oak floors, the Calacatta marble, and the unlacquered brass were enough to make a statement while not overdoing the design. As in most of my work, sometimes it's the mix of simple elements that creates the statement. In this case, four beautiful and timeless design elements complemented each other perfectly for a more traditional but forever-amazing look.

Over in "his" master bathroom, we designed a more modern and unique larger reeded, or slatted, oak vanity and surrounding cabinets. Topped with Petit Granit limestone counters and an integrated stone sink, we achieved that masculine but warm feel we were after. To further manly up the space, we made a custom steel shower door with an operable transom window for steam ventilation. We decided to fully clad the shower in slabs of Calacatta marble, which made our installer want to kill us, but which came out perfectly. Last but not least, we used Waterworks unlacquered brass plumbing fixtures like jewelry to top off this perfectly outfitted space.

Consistent flow in the design played a big part while we designed this home. In this "her" master bathroom, we used the same materials as we did in the kitchen: white oak cabinetry, Calacatta marble, and unlacquered brass plumbing. The simplicity of these materials elevated the space entirely.

ABOVE   This shower is framed with Calacatta marble and a custom brass door and features zellige tile and a beautiful Waterworks showerhead.

OPPOSITE   We wanted this bathroom to feel timeless while boasting a cool, getaway-from-it-all vibe. We chose a Calacatta marble bath, delicate linen roman shade, and banana fiber pendant light to soften up the entire space.

ABOVE Over in "his" bathroom, we designed a fully cladded Calacatta marble shower, Waterworks unlacquered brass fixtures, and a custom steel door.

OPPOSITE We went a bit more modern with the vanity, which was a scaled-up version of "her" reeded oak cabinetry (see page 275). By pairing it with Petit Granit limestone counter (the same material we used in parts of the kitchen), we achieved the overall masculine and modern feel we wanted.

RIGHT These reclaimed club chairs and wine tables transport you to an old underground speakeasy: exactly where I'd drink a bottle of wine (or two).

OPPOSITE This entryway was quite the jaw-dropping mixing of elements. From the modern Lindsey Adelman light fixture to several vintage touches, the mix of old and new made you feel a special warmth as soon as you walked through these doors.

The process of sourcing the décor took up a lot—and I mean *a lot*—of time. We weren't going to settle on catalog pieces or on items bought at any old store. While painstakingly sourcing the perfect vintage pieces and then customizing them to adorn this home, we never lost sight of the overall vision. We exercised great consideration for every fabric, color, material, pattern, and texture chosen. In the end, vintage pieces peppered every room of the home—from Pierre Jeanneret chairs in the dining room to a Bruno Mathsson vintage leather lounge chair and a hundred-year-old apothecary cabinet in the living room.

RIGHT The bedroom is surrounded by the most insanely gorgeous backyard garden, so we took advantage of the space next to the windows and installed a seating area. We used a Chautauqua Bench from Shoppe Amber Interiors as a table so my clients could prop up their feet on something soft.

OPPOSITE This master bedroom is all about the comfortable layers. We incorporated lots of warm earth tones, a mixture of textures, a collection of vintage pieces, and a crazy-cool rug that grounded the entire room.

Finding rare and conversation-worthy pieces for Bu Round Two was important. There were one-of-a-kind vintage Indian kanthas in the most beautiful patterns and colors draped over benches and rich, heavy textural linens used to make slip-covered sofas and custom sectionals. On that seating, we styled some of the prettiest pillows I have ever seen. (As in a lot of our projects, I grappled with keeping them for myself, but, as always, I ultimately decided the textiles would look much better in my client's home than in my own.) All this is to say, the finished home was one of the most eclectic and elegant mixes of layers and colors we have ever used—and for that, this will be one of my pet projects of all time.

ON THAT NOTE . . .

One of the biggest compliments I get is when you guys tell me that you took something from one of my designs and incorporated it into your homes. Even if it was as simple as discovering a new paint color or noticing a cabinet detail for the first time, knowing that something I have said or implied has made an impression is the best feeling ever. I quite literally live and breathe design, so sharing it gives me great joy. Interior design has been a huge part of my story and has made me happy for as long as I can remember. If you learn anything at all from this book, I feel like I succeeded in what I set out to do . . . which is to be a source of inspiration for you and your home.

So, how do I end this book and summarize all that we just talked about in a nutshell without sounding redundant or cheesy? I think the best way is the only way I know how. Honor the fact that I am a little quirky, a lot obsessed, and so very, very grateful for the opportunity to share this huge part of who I am with you.

My favorite part of design is that it's always evolving; our styles and aesthetics can and should change as we do. The process of design is meant to be a good time and will only ever be as fun as what you make of it. The experience you had creating your space—be it playing a game of furniture Tetris or swimming through a sea of endless options of white paint swatches—should be memorable. When you make sure to pour a bit of yourself into your surroundings and honor how important loving your space is, the result will always be perfect.

This is the end of the book, and my hope is that you have been inspired enough from these pages that you will feel confident to add your special touches to every nook, every shelf, and every cranny of your home until it makes you smile. Your design and décor journey doesn't have to be hard, but it does have to be inspired. Keep on trekking on, my friends, and I'll continue to do the same!

ACKNOWLEDGMENTS

Flipping through the pages of this book can be done in mere minutes, however every project featured in the photographs herein involved months, sometimes years, of creative work. It goes without saying that it takes a small army to pull it all together, and at the risk of sounding trite and cliché, I could not do any of this without my village! I want to give thanks to so many people, and there are a few who had a very particular hand in publishing my first book. It has been an amazing honor and an absolute dream to work with all of you. I am forever grateful.

Cat "Kitty" Chen, I doubt that when you were hired as the marketing director for Amber Interiors, you ever thought your job would evolve to coauthoring a book with me. I will never forget when we were talking about getting a ghost writer, and you looked at me and said "or, I can do it!" I thought you were crazy, and you thought I was crazy, but we jumped in headfirst and you rose to the challenge like only you could. We are the same brain, you and me, and the love and respect I have for you knows no bounds. Thank you for working harder than ever to make this book happen. None of this would have come together the way it had without you. I love you!

Tessa Neudstadt, you were the first photographer I reached out to when I had a project to share, and years and years later you are the only photographer I reach out to! Girl, we are still going strong, and I so appreciate how you manage to capture what my crappy iPhone pics never could. Thank you for entertaining the "ol' up and down" and always making my work shine. Love ya!

A big, big thank-you to the incredible team at DBA, who, for years, have been my biggest cheerleaders. I owe so much to you and could not have gotten this far without your support. Raina, you are the brightest star and whatever you say I will do. April, thank you for understanding my message so well and for believing in me so much!

Nicole Tourtelot, thank you for going to bat for me so hard. I had not one single clue what I was doing when approached to do this book, and you managed to keep me feeling like my opinion on things I knew nothing about mattered. Thank you, too, for being so supportive and believing that I had what it takes to make a book happen!

Angelin Borsics, your support and guidance has lead me through the toughest times during this process. Thanks for teaching Cat and me how to write a book. Working with you has been a joy. And to the rest of the team at Clarkson Potter, even though we haven't met, please know how grateful I am for your hard work and handiwork in creating this book, especially Sonia Persad, for your vision of design and patience with the process; Terry Deal, for your language and grammar expertise; and Kim Tyner, for proofing every image so that it transports readers directly into the room.

C.J., how did I ever survive photoshoots without you! Even though I love to "Express My Shelf," I never knew how much I needed your guidance with my "Shelf Expression." Singing, dancing, and acting a fool is so much more fun with you around, and I am so grateful to have worked with you on this book. Your floral work is a thing of great beauty, and so is your friendship. Thank you for everything, Carl John—love you big time!

To the Amber Interior Design Dream Team: I have said it before and I will say it again, I am forever in debt to you for your hard work, day in and day out, making all of our projects a reality. You each possess a unique and amazing strength, and, most important, a great energy and spirit that you bring to every project. Thanks for being the best of the best.

Thank you to my clients for bringing me into your lives and giving me the great responsibility of creating your homes. I love and appreciate you all so much.

Mom, Dad, Ryan, and Lyndsie, you have stuck by me and supported me from day one. Mama, you saw the unique nature of my very specific personality, and you nurtured it. You saw I needed to focus on having a creative outlet, and you encouraged it, teaching me how to harness that energy and grow. You always made me feel that my shortcomings were gifts, and your unwavering love fills me up.

Daddio, no matter what crazy idea I had, or how challenging I was as a teenager, you always encouraged me to press on. You helped foster my entrepreneurial spirit and always pushed me to do better. Be it in work or in life, your drive was contagious, and from watching you I learned so much about working hard and achieving the unthinkable.

Ryan and Lyndsie, I simply love you both more than I could ever describe. The laughter and the shared humor only we could understand and knowing that I was blessed with best friends as siblings are the greatest gifts of all. Thank you both for putting up with all my antics. I love you both so much.

Mike, Ducky, you have never not believed I was capable of every single thing I said we would or could do. To look back on our life and see everything we have done together makes the next chapter that much more exciting. Thank you for your patience, your support, and for being everything I need in a soul partner. I could not love you more if I tried. It's you and me and our little girl, and that's all we will ever need. The rest is just a bonus. I love you.

Gwyneth, my baby, you are the center of my entire universe. All that I do or have ever done has been with you at the core of it. Even before you chose me to be your mama, and before we met, every step I took was for you. I hope when you read through this book, you get a glimpse of why I have worked so hard all these years. I hope my work makes you proud, and I hope as you get older it inspires you to find something you love to do and make it part of your life. I love you with all my heart, precious one.

ABOUT THE AUTHOR

Amber Lewis, founder of the firm Amber Interiors and
Shoppe Amber Interiors, designs homes with a distinct
laid-back style. She lives with her husband and daughter
in Los Angeles, California. Visit her blog at allsortsof.com,
and follow her on Instagram @AmberInteriors.